With the Camel Corps
Up the Nile

A MEMBER OF THE CAMEL CORPS.

With the Camel Corps
Up the Nile
The 'Gordon Relief Expedition'
Against the Mahdists, Sudan, 1885

Edward Gleichen

LEONAUR

With the Camel Corps Up the Nile: the 'Gordon Relief Expedition'
Against the Mahdists, Sudan, 1885
by Edward Gleichen

Originally published in 1888 under the title
With the Camel Corps Up the Nile

Leonaur is an imprint of Oakpast Ltd

Material original to this edition and
presentation of text in this form
copyright © 2009 Oakpast Ltd

ISBN: 978-1-84677-910-7 (hardcover)
ISBN: 978-1-84677-909-1 (softcover)

http://www.leonaur.com

Publisher's Notes

The views expressed in this book are not necessarily
those of the publisher.

Contents

Preface   7

Formation of the Camel Corps   9

From Assiut to Assouan   17

Journey to Dongola   27

Ghosts in the Desert   34

Marketing at Abu Gussi   38

The Marines Arrive   42

Abu Halfa and the Mahdists   48

Building Forts   58

Advance of the Column   67

The Enemy in Sight   71

Night of the 16th   77

Action of Abu Klea   81

A Terrible Night-March   90

Action of Abu Kru   96

Back to the Zeriba   104

Gordon's Troops Arrive   108

Outpost Duty   113

On the March Again   120

Kababish   126

The End of the Relief Expedition   131

Retirement on Gakdul   135

Robbers on the Road   141

A Private Battle   146

Prospects of an Autumn Campaign   152

Life at Dongola   157

Dog-Hunting   162

Conflagrations   166

Orders to Quit   169

Wady Halfa   174

Alexandria and Home   181

Appendices   187

Preface

In presenting the following pages to the public, I feel that a certain apology is due, for it is now over three years since the Nile Expedition took place (and most people have forgotten all about it), and several accounts of it, infinitely better and fuller than mine, have been published.

To tell the truth, my story was about to see the light two years ago, and it was only owing to circumstances over which I had not much control that its appearance has been delayed till now.

Another thing, this book does not profess to be anything more than what its title proclaims it to be, namely, a record of what the Camel Corps, and more especially the Guards' Camel Regiment, saw and did up the Nile in 1884-85. I have, therefore, not attempted to describe things I did not see, and have purposely avoided "cribbing" from other people's books on the same subject.

Thirdly, I must crave the merciful indulgence of my readers for the pictures; all I have to urge on their behalf is that they represent real incidents, for the original sketches were done out there.

Lastly, I shall be most grateful if any one will point out to me any inaccuracies in the work, for my aim has been to present not a fanciful, but a true picture of what occurred.

One thing more, the initials referring to officers of the G.C.R. are, in nearly every case, those of their nicknames, not their surnames.

G

Chapter 1

Formation of the Camel Corps

One day in September, 1884, on coming off one of those numerous guards in Dublin that make a subaltern's life a burden to him, I found the joyful news awaiting me that I was to go out to the Soudan at once with the Camel Corps detachment of my battalion.

As everybody knows, this sudden despatch of troops to the Nile was due to the Government having suddenly taken into its head the idea that it was necessary to rescue General Gordon from his perilous position at Khartoum, which he had held since the previous February. "Better late than never;" accordingly an expedition was equipped to proceed up the river, in pursuance of a determination which ought to have been carried out at least three months earlier.

The idea had only recently been started that, in order to allow of troops acting with any success up the Nile, it was absolutely necessary that a certain proportion of them should be mounted on camels, both for facility of transport across the desert (if necessary) to Khartoum, and for rapidity of action. Accordingly a Camel Corps was organised, drawn half from the Cavalry and half from the Infantry.

The Cavalry part was to be composed of detachments from all the Cavalry regiments in Great Britain at the time, subdivided into "Heavies" and "Lights;" the Infantry part of detachments from the Brigade of Guards and from the regiments already out in Egypt,

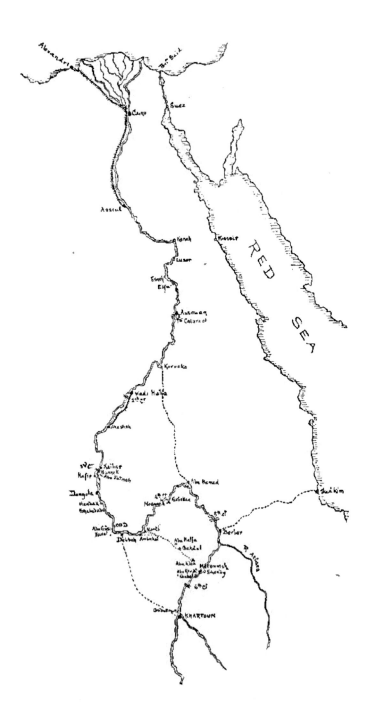

these last to go by the name of (Camel) Mounted infantry.

Each detachment was to consist of 2 officers, 2 sergeants, 2 corporals, 1 bugler (or trumpeter), and 38 men. The "Heavies" numbered 10 detachments, from the 1st and 2nd Life Guards, Blues, Bays, 4th and 5th Dragoon Guards, Royals, Scots Greys, 5th and 16th Lancers: total, 23 officers and 431 men.

The "Lights," from the 3rd, 4th, 7th, 10th, 11th, 15th, 18th, 20th, and 21st Hussars, numbered (9 detachments) 21 officers and 388 men. The Guards numbered 7 detachments, from the 1st, 2nd, and 3rd battalions Grenadiers, 1st and 2nd Coldstream, and 1st and 2nd Scots Guards: total, 17 officers and 302 men. Each of these divisions, Heavies, Lights, and Guards, had (included above) a staff of Commanding Officer, Adjutant and Quartermaster, and Surgeon. The grand total that left England was therefore 61 officers and 1,121 men. The men had all to be marksmen, or first-class shots, twenty-two years old at least, of course medically fit, and of as good character as possible. In fact, they were as good men as could be got anywhere, and a finer shipload than those on board the *Deccan* never left England. The Mounted Infantry, whom we were to join in Egypt, were somewhat differently constituted, and numbered altogether about 25 officers and 480 men.[1]

Not much time was lost in getting our outfit, for the orders were to start in four days. Needless to say, this playful order was only meant to hurry the department up a bit that did the clothing and arming, and the "Guards' Camel Regiment" stood fully armed and accoutred four days before we actually started.

As people remarked at the time, the men's costume looked more like the seventeenth than the nineteenth century, the bandoliers, breeches, and stocking-like putties giving them a look of the last Civil war. The men were clothed in red serge "jumpers" (or loose tunics), yellow-ochre cord breeches, dark blue putties (or leg-bandages), and white pith helmets. Their arms and accoutrements were rifle, sword-bayonet, bandolier (of brown leather worn over the left shoulder, and holding fifty cartridges),

---

1. See Appendix I. for names and details.

brown belt, pouch, frog and sling, haversack and water-bottle; also brown ankle-boots. That was what appeared outwardly. Inwardly, in their ordinary valise, were sundries in the shape of a grey serge jumper (always worn in Egypt), goggles, veil, drawers, cholera-belt, Prayer Book, housewife, spurs (which were never once used), spare pair of boots, shirts, socks, and all the usual paraphernalia of a man's kit. Officers were dressed much the same, except that they generally wore long field-boots instead of putties; their arms being, of course, sword and revolver, attached to a brown leather belt with shoulder-braces. I forgot to mention another peculiar article carried by the men, namely, a Namaqua rifle-bucket, for attaching to the saddle, the rifle being placed in it butt foremost.

At length, after several alterations had been made as to the ships and dates we were to sail by, we found ourselves embarked at Portsmouth on the 26th September in the P. and O. *Deccan*, together with the Heavies, some 130 stronger than ourselves. With the reader's leave we'll skip all the leave-takings and farewells, and consider ourselves started.

Of course everybody was cheerful the first day, and of course nearly everybody was ill the second, but this is only the usual fate of man. The men would look on it all as a big spree, and were quite aggrieved at first if you punished them for "small reports." However, finding that the officers didn't see it in the same light as themselves, they wisely accepted their fate, and discipline like that of a barracks reigned in the ship.

Being sick and getting over it occupied three days, but after that there was next to nothing to do, beyond shooting. The beneficent Government had given us sixty rounds per man, to shoot off before we reached Alexandria, but had forgotten to supply us with targets. We accordingly shot everything shootable to pieces, straw targets, old floating boxes, bottles free, bottles tied, and bottles astern, till we were reduced to shooting paper, and finally foam, or an occasional whale or porpoise. The Heavies and ourselves being dressed alike, we amused ourselves by cutting out red cloth badges and letters to distinguish the various corps, such as: 1GG (1st Grenadiers), RHG (Blues), 5L (5th Lancers), and so on; these were sewn on the right arm.

Our evenings were enlivened by concerts of all sorts, but no incident worthy of remark occurred till we were passing Malta, and signalled for the latest news. "Defend cook gone Cairo," was all we got, and this unravelled meant seemingly: "Guards' cook," etc., referring to a Mai tee who had been wired for to act in that capacity. There was no word "Guards" in the signal code, so they used the nearest approach to it. No further news of any sort did we get till we reached Alexandria harbour on the 7th October, early, when the first report was that we were probably to go back to England in two days, as the Mahdi and all his sheikhs had caved in! The whole battalion, however, while awaiting definite orders, went ashore to stretch their legs for a march round the town, and there we first met our future steeds, sloping along under their loads of corn and stuffs.

They looked rather meagre beasts to carry us, but we were consoled by "one who knew" telling us that riding camels were entirely superior to that sort of animal.

Everyone knows or has read what Alexandria looks like, so I will only remark that it is exactly like what you expect to see,

FIRST VIEW OF OUR FUTURE STEEDS.

but not so hot and a good deal cleaner.

On returning to harbour we found the Canadian voyageurs had arrived. As two had deserted before starting, and they were an undisciplined lot, we "found" a small guard over them. This, however, turned out to be quite unnecessary, as they were in high spirits and had no evil intentions whatever of bolting. Their clothes did not seem suited to the climate, being thick grey tweed and black shiny hats, but they were served out with helmets as soon as practicable. Many of them were Indians, a few only spoke French, and a good many had never been in a boat before, being bankers' clerks, storekeepers, cow-boys, anything even old soldiers who had been out in '82, and come back to see if the country had changed. Whatever their previous characters or situations had been, there was no doubt they were in high glee at their outing, and anxious to get up to the front as soon as possible.

The fact of the Canadians being sent up river it once went far to destroy the dismal report of our laving to go back immediately, and, as it proved, we were disembarked next morning, in our grey "jumpers" (which we wore ever after), and packed off to the Red Barracks for the day, to start for Cairo that evening. The first companies of the Heavies and ourselves were sent off as advanced party, train to start at six. Eventually the train moved slowly out of the station at 8.15, and we dawdled along till about midnight, when we were shunted to make way for a train behind us; we sleepily looked at the passing train, and beheld—the rest of the battalion! They got to Cairo two hours before us, we not arriving till 8.30; over twelve hours going 120 miles! We found the G.C.R. (Guards' Camel Regiment) quartered in the Kasr en Nil, a formerly beautiful palace, belonging to Arabi, but which had since been turned into barracks for the 49th (Berkshire).

The next report was that there wouldn't be room for us in Cairo, and we were to remain at the Pyramids under canvas for the next week or so. Accordingly we packed up again, and started early next morning (the 10th) to march there. It was rather warm work, and tantalising too. Between the Pyramids and the town is a large area of low-lying ground, covered with water in the time of high Nile (just when we were there); across this runs a causeway, bordered with sycamores, straight on end for nearly five miles, the Pyramids at the end of it. The air is so clear that the Pyramids seem not a mile off, yet you walk, and walk, and walk, and seem to get no nearer.

At last we got there, and proceeded to pitch our camp of Indian mountain service tents. The sand was loose and deep the pegs would not hold; puff came a little wind, up went the pegs, and over went the tent. The only way was to scrape away a hole bury the pegs in that, and stamp down the sand if possible. Flies in myriads, hot sun, baggage to haul over this infernal sand up to the axle-trees. No matter; we shook down quickly, and dinner restored our equanimity. There we remained for a week, heliographing to Cairo for "shaves," which arrived in great variety, and exploring the Pyramids and temples in the neighbourhood. The Heavies were quartered with us at the Pyramids, and, much to our envy, received their marching orders on the 13th.

At length we got the order to move, and moved, on the 16th, from the Boulak Dacrour Station by night to Assiut. The heat was something appalling, and not a chink could we open of any sort; for then we were suffocated with the dust that rose in clouds round the train: the Black Hole must have been a joke

ROAD TO THE PYRAMIDS.

15

MORNING TOILET AT THE PYRAMIDS.

to it. There were only three of us in a third-class carriage, so two tried to sleep on the seats, while the third reposed on the floor; the latter was occasionally disturbed by one of the upper occupants falling on top of him, so at last we gave up attempting to sleep, and wished for the day. It came at last, and we arrived about nine o'clock at Assiut, where the railway ended. We therefore proceeded to detrain, and embarked the men on two barges, which were lashed together, and towed by a sort of penny steamer; this latter the officers inhabited.

CHAPTER 2

From Assiut to Assouan

I had been led to expect beautiful scenery on the Nile, but anything more uninteresting I never saw. The river was much broader and infinitely dirtier than I could have thought; in fact, if you let the water in your bath lie for two minutes, there was a thick deposit of mud at once.

All along the banks were unending forests of *dhurra* corn, beans, cotton, and all sorts of native grain; no coffee, no sugar, and no tobacco, which sadly disappointed me, as I was looking forward to unlimited supplies of these articles for daily consumption. Mud—liquid, soft, and hard—and green crops, with distant views of very hot-looking blue and pink rocks were our daily landscape for eleven days, the monotony being occasionally varied by palms and mud villages. At night we anchored off either bank, as the captain refused to go on in the dark, for fear of mud-banks.

Our chief amusement was going on shore in the evenings, and buying chickens, eggs, vegetables, and milk. The average price was—melon, one *piastre* (2½d.); eggs, ten a *piastre*; turkey, half-a-crown; and goose, eighteen-pence.

Before long we formulated these rules, and it was only by sticking rigidly to them that we managed to get things moderately cheap:

1. Always bring a *koorbash* or a stick with you.
2. Bargain in the dark, so as to pass off your bad *piastres*.
3. Always get the article desired into your possession before you attempt to haggle.

4. Offer never more than half what they ask, and go away if you do not get it at your price; they will then follow you and conform to your wishes.

The day before getting to Assouan we passed a disabled steamer and two barges, on which were the "Lights." We sympathised outwardly with them, but inwardly were much pleased that they had broken their crank, as that meant we should probably take their place, and be first to go up country.

And so it turned out. On arriving at Assouan, on the 28th, we found orders for the three first companies[1] to go on, by the first steamer available, to Wady Halfa, there to receive our camels and equipments, and proceed up to Dongola. As we were not to start till next day, two or three of us strolled into the town, which was much like all the other towns we had passed, only larger and somewhat more unsweet, and then went to see a troop of the Egyptian Camel Corps go through their evolutions. What struck us most was the extreme ease with which the beasts were guided only some half-dozen having nose-reins. They advanced in companies, wheeled into line, sections right, front formed, in fact, did everything they had to do with the greatest precision, and even proceeded to skirmish. If Egyptians do their manoeuvres so well, said we, what won't the "Brigade" do?

Next day we trained to Philae, about seven miles round the first cataract, and went on board our steamer. Though the country, so far, had been the reverse of lovely, the view from Shellal, the head of the cataract, looking downstream with the island and ruined temples of Philae in the foreground, was quite beautiful; the towering gates of the big temple, the graceful pillars of the little one overhanging the foaming water some eighty feet sheer, with the cataract tearing between the wild black rocks in the background, formed the most beautiful piece of scenery we had yet seen on the river. By moonlight it was still prettier.

The steamer we found ourselves on was much larger than the last; in fact, it was the Khedive's own, and towed, besides the two large barges for our men, some twenty whalers, wherein

---

1. i.e. 1st Grenadiers, 1st Coldstream, and 1st Scots.

were stowed part of the 56th (Essex). Nothing much occurred worthy of remark during this voyage, except the shooting of a large crocodile by one of us.

It was on a hot Sunday afternoon, when, on turning a bend in the river, not far from the wonderful temple of Abu Simbl, the Arab in the bows shouted that there was a big crocodile asleep on a mud-bank in the middle of the river. B—— accordingly got his rifle, and, as the awakening brute slid lazily into the water, plumbed him under the right shoulder at a distance of quite 130 yards a first-rate shot. The beast stopped at the water's edge, and began to lash his flaily tail about. By this time the excitement amongst the sailors was immense; the sporting old captain stopped the steamer, a boat was manned, and we pulled off to the bank, I having charge of the rifle wherewith to finish him. He was already half in the water, and the difficulty was to get his head out, to let me have a fair shot at his eye which, I had learnt in my youthful days, was his only vulnerable point. The boat-hook was the only instrument to haul him back by, so half-a-dozen niggers manned it, hooked it into a corner of his jaw, and tugged his great head round for the *coup de grace*. Even with a second bullet in the place where his brain ought to have been, he had life enough to snap at the boat-hook with such force as to leave marks of his teeth on the iron head. A third shot close under the eye finished him, and with much labour he was hoisted into the boat, and from thence on to the steamer. On measuring him, he was found to be a couple of inches under thirteen feet a real monster. When we halted for good that evening, the carcase was skinned and devoured (entrails and all) by some natives from a neighbouring village. B—— took possession of the hide, and put it on the paddle-box to dry in the sun. When the wind was ahead the stench was really grand, and drove us off the after-deck.

That same evening we resolved to go and have a look at Abu Simbl, which lay about a mile and a half downstream. We pulled down easily enough in an unloaded whaler, and landed at once. Though we had caught a glimpse of the temple from the steam-

THE COUP-DE-GRACE

er, its full grandeur did not strike us till we had got close up to it. The peculiarity of it is that the whole thing is cut out of the solid limestone rock, with a doorway only some 8 feet broad by 15 high. The interior dimensions are about 90 by 50, by 45 feet high, the walls and ceiling covered with hieroglyphics. Guarding the entrance are four colossal seated figures (also cut out of the rock), representing Rameses II. As each figure if standing up would measure over 60 feet high, the immense and solid grandeur of the whole can be imagined. After gazing at the interior with the help of a small piece of magnesium light (which only lasted three and a half seconds), we tore ourselves away and tried to pull back upstream. I say "tried," for after a quarter of an hour's hard pulling against a fearful current, we found ourselves some yards further downstream than when we started. If eight men pulling an empty boat proceed minus three yards in fifteen minutes, low long would it take ten men to pull up the Nile in a boat loaded to the gunwale with stores and men? Such was the rule-of-three sum that presented itself. We had ignominiously, therefore, to disembark and tow from the shore, and eventually arrived at the steamer very late for dinner.

The following day we arrived at Wady Halfa, having done the distance from Assouan (180 miles) in four days.

Wady Halfa, though marked on all maps as a town, is really nothing of the sort. There are (or rather were, when we arrived) ten or twelve mud hovels, but besides these there are none but buildings connected with the railway, which starts from here and at that time finished thirty-five miles off, somewhere n the desert. This is the identical railway begun by Ismail on the right bank of the river, and intended to communicate with Khartoum. Would that Gordon had not put a stop to this magnificent enterprise, as he did when he was Governor of the Soudan, in '79! If it had only been continued as far as Dongola, what a different ending there would have been to the expedition! Wady Halfa to Dongola that was the chief natural obstacle the river difficult of navigation, and making an unnecessarily large bend (in fact, three sides of a square instead of straight across); besides this, two formidable cataracts and many other smaller ones. The land journey on camels was also very tedious, taking eleven days or more to do the 235 miles, whereas a railway would have shot troops and stores across in a couple of days at the outside. It was a great pity.

The first few days at Wady Halfa we spent in pitching our camp, drilling on foot *a la* Mounted Infantry (all by sections), taking over equipments and saddles, mending and strengthening ditto, and lastly taking over our camels. There were two patterns of saddles, one the knifeboard, and the other the Mounted Infantry pattern. The authorities couldn't make up their minds which to serve us out with, so after issuing and recalling the saddles two or three times, they compromised matters by giving the men the knifeboard, and the officers the other pattern. The knifeboard pattern is constructed thus: Imagine framework composed of two wooden frames about 24 in. by 15, transversely strengthened, and lashed together along one long side so as to form an angle of 60° with each other. No; it is hopeless to try to describe it, it looks like this:

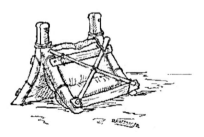

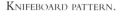

KNIFEBOARD PATTERN.   MOUNTED INFANTRY PATTERN.

The M.I. pattern is much the same, only stronger and heavier, and the seat pear-shaped, made of iron. Under the framework are two cushions, so stuffed as to make room for the hump of the camel. Over the framework are hung the girths, stirrups, and a pair of saddle-bags, or *zuleetahs*, of canvas and red leather, which amply contain all your kit; on the near side is strapped a rolled blanket and waterproof sheet, on the off a *tente d'abri* to every two men. The Namaqua rifle-bucket is attached to the off rear side of the framework, and secured by passing the long strap under the belly of the animal, over the two girths, and buckling it on the near side to a buckle nailed on for the purpose. On the after pommel is hung the leather water-skin, or *gerbah* (of which more hereafter), with sometimes an apron of thin leather below, to keep it off the quarters of the camel, or above, to protect it from the sun, and the Egyptian water-bottle or *mussek*, a long stiff leather bottle, which, unless it lets it all leak out in half-an-hour, makes the water beautifully cool. On the fore pommel hangs the camel's rations for three days, thirty pounds of corn. Over the saddle-bags are placed the second blanket, and over everything comes a padded red leather saddle cover, on top of which the rider is perched. Such is a camel-saddle and equipment.[2]

The knifeboard framework was made of thin pieces of un-seasoned wood, which we had to lash with wire; the girths and straps were fearfully rotten, and were only kept going by a liberal application of grease; whilst the water-skins and *musseks* were heartbreaking, letting out the water nearly as soon as filled. We were told they would swell when wet, and thus close up the pores, and in some cases they did, though in others they were holey; generally as soon as one hole was sewn up, another would open, and the water would trickle steadily out; it also escaped invisibly, I suppose through evaporation. What would happen if we had to depend on them for our lives, we didn't know, but didn't trouble our heads about it, thinking we should stick to the Nile most of the way.

The equipment ready, the next step was to get our camels, which were visible about a mile off, at the camel depot. The sight was an extraordinary one: rows upon rows upon rows of camels, baggagers and *hygeems* (riding camels), of every size, colour, and description, from the enormous heavy rhinoceros-skinned transport beast to the small well-bred trotter, only used for posting and despatches. They came from all parts, the Delta, Aden, Kosseir, Dongola, and even from Arabia. These last were few and far between, being chosen for their swiftness, and con-

---

2. See Appendix II.

sequently very valuable. Their pace is so smooth, that the test at the Meccan Tattersall's is for the rider to carry a full cup of coffee at full trot; if he spills any, it is considered that the animal is under-bred. The Delta camels were the weakest, though not the smallest, whilst the steeds selected for us came mostly from the parts round about. They were a nice-looking set of beasts, and we were of course very particular to have the pick of the lot; sore-backed ones were exchanged, and camel after camel sent back for (sometimes imaginary) weaknesses, till the officer in charge vowed he'd exchange no more.

The next thing was to fit the saddles, and much trouble ensued, as no two camels are humped exactly alike; that done, we mounted our beasts with some difficulty, and manoeuvred a bit in line, the camels acting as if they had never done anything else all their lives. Their headgear was simple, a black leather headstall, the rein being a rope about seven feet long, attached to an iron curb-chain under the lower lip, no part of the headgear in the mouth; by this, passing on the left side of the neck, you could pull him to the left, or press it against his neck, making him go to the right; it also served as a rope for tethering or knee-lashing him.[3]

The men were highly delighted with their first mount, and proceeded to trot and canter their steeds all over the plain, although a camel's anatomy is not constructed for the purpose of cantering; many were the croppers they came, especially when getting up, v but it only made them the keener.

Mounting a frisky camel is exciting work for the beginner, and nearly always results in a cropper. The mode of procedure should be thus: having made your camel to kneel by clearing your throat loudly at him and tugging at his rope, shorten your rein till you bring his head round to his shoulder, put your foot in the stirrup, and throw your leg over. With his head jammed like that, he cannot rise, and must wait till you give him his head.

---

3. i.e. tying his near foreleg (bent) to his neck when kneeling. Double knee-lashing is accomplished by tying his neck to both forelegs when in the same position, thus making him quite helpless—not so easy as it sounds, especially with a restless animal.

A BOLTER.

Unless you do as directed, he will get up before your leg is over; if this happens, stand in the stirrup till he is up, and then throw your leg over, otherwise you will infallibly meet with a hideous catastrophe. We found that with the rifle in the bucket it was impossible to get one's leg over, so always made the men pass the sling of the rifle over their left wrists before getting on. After a time we found it easier to stand alongside and give a big heave of the right leg over the saddle without touching the near stirrup at all. So much for mounting; dismounting is, of course, the same reversed.

We had the fact repeatedly impressed on us that we were not to be used as cavalry at all, that we were never to fight on our camels, and in fact that they were only to be used as means of rapid transport from one place to another. Accordingly, we did not tire our beasts by trotting for long distances. Although they could carry a native so for a long time, it was different when they had on their back a thirteen stone man, with all his kit and paraphernalia, and their own rations besides. The average weight must have been about 340lb., distributed as under:

	lb
Man	165
120 Rounds	12
Rifle, etc	9
Forage	30
Kit	30
Rations	6
Water	40
Blankets, etc	20
Saddle	30
Total	342lb

The first thing to do when we had learnt to stick on the camels, was obviously to learn how to use them; but the system of drill was not perfected till some time after, every colonel or general under whose command we came having different ideas on the subject. So meanwhile we studied Mounted Infantry Drill, which subsequently we had all to unlearn again, as the idea in that drill is for one man to hold four horses, whilst the three remaining men of his section skirmish around; this was, we subsequently found, although not impossible, quite inapplicable to our particular steeds, and accordingly left it off after a short time, waiting for the issue of a regulation "Camel Drill."

CHAPTER 3

Journey to Dongola

At length, on the 12th November, we got our orders to proceed the next morning to Dongola (235 miles) per camel-back, and started accordingly. Of the other four companies of the G.C.R. that we had left at Assouan, two (the 2nd Grenadiers and 2nd Coldstream detachments) received their camels there, and were marching up, and the other two were to follow by steamer to Wady Halfa, receive their camels there, and all come on together. Both the Heavy and the Light Camel Corps were still at Assouan, waiting for their camels. We heard a rumour that the only reason why we were sent up first was, because the only saddles yet ready were the light knifeboard pattern, which was too light for the Heavies. The Lights had not turned up at Assouan as soon as was expected, owing to their broken crank, so accordingly we were sent. How far this report was true I never inquired.

Besides our three companies starting from Wady Halfa, we had a small train of baggage camels, a section of the Field Hospital, under a first-rate doctor (Briggs—the same who afterwards attended poor Sir Herbert), and a few extras in the shape of Commissariat and Transport men.

At last we felt something like "business," and bade *adieu* with no regrets to civilisation in the shape of steamers and railways. Our road lay more or less along the Nile the whole way, the detachment encamping on the river at night, at settled stations, and making an average of twenty miles during the day. As one day was very much like another, I will only describe the usual mode of procedure. Starting at five or six in the morning, according to the distance to be done, we walked, dragging our camels after us, for four or five miles in the cool of the morning. When the sun got hot (which it did unpleasantly soon) we mounted and rode, with only half-an-hour's interval at noon, straight on end for eight or nine hours. Walking like this is most fearfully monotonous, and it's no use hurrying the camel up; he simply *won't* hurry. On he goes at his two-and-three-quarter miles an hour pace, with sickening regularity; and beyond keeping the men in their proper places there is absolutely nothing whatever to do. I tried reading, I tried writing no good; the only thing in which I met with any success was going to sleep. After a time we all trained ourselves to sleep in the saddle for short periods generally very short, as we fell off at the slightest irregularity of pace. However, any excitement was better than nodding in the hot sun for hours, only rousing yourself to abuse your camel for not going faster, and your men for not keeping together. We adopted all sorts of formation on the march, according to the ground we came to: column of companies, fours, two deep, or even single file over some of the rocky passes.

The word "desert" presented to my mind's eye an "illimitable waste of burning sand, with neither rock nor tree whereon to rest the weary eye." But not once the whole time I was out did I see anything answering to that description. Generally speaking, the desert was composed of low, rocky black hills and hard gravel, with occasional dried-up tufts of long grass and low dry scrub of all sorts. Sometimes the ground was so mountainous that we had to dismount and lead our camels, but on emerging on to a *khor* (or dried-up watercourse, one or two miles broad—*I* should call it a plain) the ground was generally hard sand, often gravelly, and always good walking.

On the stony places I really pitied the podgy, soft-looking feet of the camels, but they knocked their toes against the sharp stones with the greatest unconcern. I also once had practical experience that their feet are not soft, by a violent kick I received

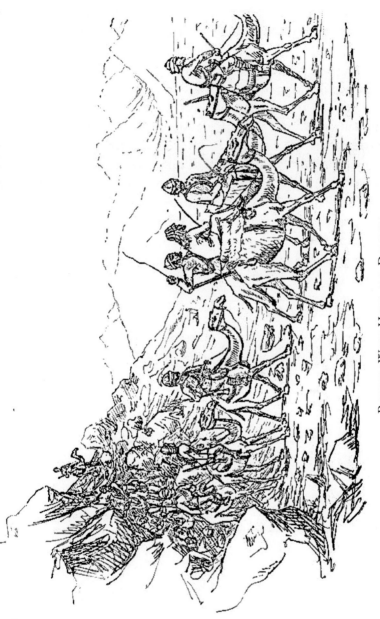

Between Wady Halfa and Dongola

from the hind-leg of a camel, who thought himself insulted by my examining his head-stall in the dark. A camel's hind-legs will reach anywhere over his head, round his chest, and on to his hump; even when lying down, an evil-disposed animal will shoot out his legs, and bring you to a sitting posture. His neck is of the same pliancy.

He will chew the root of his tail, nip you in the calf, or lay the top of his head on his hump. He also bellows and roars at you, whatever you are doing saddling him, feeding him, mounting him, unsaddling him. To the uninitiated, a camel going for one with his mouth open and gurgling horribly is a terrifying spectacle; but do not mind him, it is only his way. He hardly ever bites, but when he does you feel it for some time; as a matter of fact we only once had a man laid up from a bite in the hand, but he had to go into hospital for it. I heard of one or two men having a leg broken from a kick at various

"GET UP, YOU BRUTE."

times, but it was the exception, and not the rule, for a camel is really a very docile animal, and learns to behave himself in the most trying positions with equanimity, though I fear it is only the result of want of brains.

Regarding his wonderful powers of endurance, I was told of journeys made across country from Dongola to Alexandria (950 miles) in eight days; of his marvellous powers of going for forty days running; of trotting 200 miles without a halt; of his going fifteen days without water, etc. My experience is that he gets a sore back after four days, or less; does not go comfortably for more than five consecutive days, and as for trotting, it was only by a vigorous application of the *koorbash* that I could succeed in making mine go that pace for more than fifty yards at a time. I own that, though my first impressions of a camel's powers were thus bad, and I do not now believe in those wonderful tales told me by wily natives, yet the beast rose wonderfully in my estimation some time afterwards, when we were in the thick of "real business" in the Bayuda Desert, on seeing the patient way in which our poor camels walked on and on, with no food or water whatever inside them, till they dropped dead in their tracks; but of that hereafter.

I cherished a great affection for my own camel, named Potiphar, a great upstanding white beast of some 22 hands, who reciprocated it by bellowing every time I came near, and making playful rushes at me. I really think I succeeded in making him know and care for me after a time, for he ceased his attacks, and reduced his bellow to a grumble; but he got no further in his love than that. His pace was usually very slow, and required continual whacking, but when excited he walked away from the others; his trot was not one of his good points in fact, his chief talent lay in doing more work and breaking down less than any of the others. He carried me from Wady Halfa to Metammeh, and back to Gakdul, making two extra journeys from Gubat to Gakdul and back, and one from Gakdul to Korti and back grand total about 1,220 miles, not counting extras. During the whole time he only had a sore back three times; but I must say when I saw him last the poor beast had holes in his side you could put a cocoanut in.

This long digression about the habits of camels has led us from the point; let us return. Another mode of employing ourselves was by flag-wagging to each other. We had learnt the signalling alphabet, and one of us sitting backwards on his camel sent messages with primitive flags to the others at the rear of the column. The camel of the signaller never objected to the proceedings, even when his rider was sitting backwards. In the latter case he was generally led by a certain youthful nigger from Darfur, a slave who had escaped from his masters at Wady Halfa and joined us. One morning his enraged owners overtook us, and claimed him; however, our commanding officer, R——, made a magnificent speech about there being no slavery under the British flag, sent the Arabs to the right-about, and took possession of the boy himself, who became forthwith his devoted servant, or, perhaps I should say, his slave.

When we arrived at our halting-place we used to form column of companies, dismounting by word of command, and tether our steeds to a long cable rope brought with us for the purpose. The men then fed the camels, took their saddles off when cool, cooked and ate their own dinner, and watered the camels at the river every other day. Five pounds of grain was our steeds' allowance at the evening meal, the other five pounds being given them in the early morning, half-an-hour before starting. Great care had to be taken with the camels, as they are really delicate animals, and had all sorts of unknown ailments if carelessly looked after. When taken down to the river, some camels would look aimlessly about, exhausting the patience of the man by not drinking for ten minutes, or more, and sometimes not drinking at all if the least jostled. They used to get colds in their noses, too, at night, especially the flank ones; sometimes they caught cold if the saddles were removed too soon; some times, also, they fought in the lines, and got their ropes into fearful confusion. They used to break away at times, and wander all over the lines, causing great sorrow to their riders, who came to seek them, and they were not. Besides this, on the march a camel would occasionally go slower and slower, and at last kneel down without warning, refusing to get up; no examination would discover the seat of the sickness or injury (if any), so he was whacked till he did go on. Altogether they were a sad trouble.

Chapter 4

Ghosts in the Desert

Some days we went for more than thirty miles, at other times not more than twelve; but both men and animals were grateful for an occasional day's rest vouchsafed unto them. After a time one gets pains in the back and loins from perpetual riding; speaking for myself, I found I got very slack in the legs on dismounting, and could not sleep at all well, camels playing a large part in my frequent nightmares. This condition of affairs, though, luckily, did not last more than a week.

As I remarked before, the country was chiefly rocky and gravelly, our road leading from point to point on the river, generally straight across country. Sometimes the glimpses of the Nile were excessively pretty, sometimes uninteresting in the extreme. Although we hardly ever came across real deep sandy ground, we were given ample assurance that the "illimitable waste" business does exist in some parts of the continent. We had a capital little interpreter, Mehemet Effendi, who had travelled over most of the Soudan, and some of his stories of the desert were thrilling very. I particularly remember his describing to us the desert between Korosko and Abu Hamed, which he said was ankle-deep in loose sand the whole way (230 miles). It is the desert where Mehemet Ali lost a whole army from thirst, and their ghosts are supposed to haunt it; at all events, our friend swore that the last time he journeyed across he was disturbed at night by ghostly trumpet-calls from the desert, mingled with faint words of command and the tramp of phantom feet.

He was a well-educated man, having been brought up in

Marseilles and lived in Italy for some time; he was therefore not generally liable to his countrymen's superstitions, in fact, he owned he never believed in *djins* or spirits before; but he was perfectly certain that over and over again he saw white-coated columns in the distance, disappearing to the accompaniment of the ghostly music aforesaid This happened just in the region where their bones are now covered with the shifting sands!

Let me remark by the way that it is rash for an Upper Nile traveller to trust to the names of villages marked on the most official maps; I did, and with no result, for the natives knew not the names. Eventually I discovered that the names vary from one generation to another. It happens thus: there are no real villages at all, only districts full of isolated or clustered huts scattered here and there along the banks; the head man of the district calls it after himself, wherefore the name only lasts till he dies and the next man gets it. For instance, there is a village marked as Ras Dulgo, whereas Ras Dulgo is a district eight miles long. Again, we one day asked the way to Absarat; no one knew, as Absarat's grandson reigned in his stead, and had forgotten the name of his grandfather. Yet again, we asked the way to Faridi, and the gentleman himself was pointed out to us!

Eventually we arrived opposite Dongola on the 26th November, having been exactly a fortnight on the march, two days of which had been spent in resting at places called respectively Akasheh and Abu Fatmeh; our rate therefore averaged just twenty miles a day. Dongola is a big mud town on the left bank of the river, with, as every one knows, a Mudir, a barracks, and a post-office, and, at that time (lastly, but by no means leastly), Lord Wolseley. Many people seem not to have known which Dongola this was, as on all the maps were marked two Dongolas—Old and New; for their information, therefore, I beg to state that it was the latter. Old Dongola is no more a town than, say, Old Sarakhs in Afghanistan; it is a collection of ruins on the opposite (right) bank of the river, some sixty or seventy miles upstream, and has nothing whatever to do with the other Dongola: in fact, the sheikh of Old Dongola didn't know his ruins by that name at all.

Our orders from Wady Halfa were to cross the river at Dongola, and probably stay there to wait for the rest of the Camel Corps; but, on rowing over to the town, our commanding officer received orders not to cross for some twenty miles further. The reason of this was that smallpox had broken out in the town, and had laid low several of the Mounted Infantry and the 35th (Sussex). Accordingly next day, after having been inspected by the General, we proceeded to our crossing-place, which rejoiced in the name of Akhir.

A worse place for crossing could hardly have been chosen; the banks on one side were steep and sandy, on the other muddy and slippery. However, with much difficulty, we induced our camels to slither down the bank and into the *nuggers* ready to receive them. These *nuggers* were the ordinary boats used in those parts; very solid, one-masted, and generally equal to holding five camels. We were luckily favoured by the wind, and got all our camels (about 170) over in six hours or so. Next day saw us *en route* for the camp at Shabadud, some twenty miles further on; and much pleased were we to arrive there.

The Mounted Infantry part of the Camel Corps had arrived some four days before, and got the camp ready for Sir Herbert Stewart's brigade to collect in before starting upstream. The Brigadier-General was already there, and only waiting for the rest of the G.C.R. in order to practise a little drill, and then advance as far as Ambukol, the point settled by the Commander-in-Chief for concentration.

After repeated trials, the system of Camel Drill had been more or less perfected by Sir Herbert, and we proceeded to learn it at once. Our other four companies turned up on the 4th December, and for the next five days we were hard at it. The idea was as follows. Since we were on no account to be used as Cavalry, but simply as Infantry transported quickly on camels, the object to be aimed at was freedom of action as Infantry combined with defence of our steeds. Accordingly, the system evolved was to jam the camels into a square mass, and flank them by squares of men at one or two opposite corners; if necessary to act away from the camels, to leave simply enough men to defend them, and manoeuvre freely as Infantry.[1]

The Mounted Infantry Camel Regiment of course drilled on the same principle. During the time we were at Shabadud, we practised these formations incessantly, and after nine days were as nearly perfect as we ever expected to be.

---

1. See Appendix III. for details.

CHAPTER 5

Marketing at Abu Gussi

On the 10th December the brigade (composed of a squadron
19th Hussars, the Guards' Camel Regiment, and the Mounted Infantry) packed up and started for Ambukol, which town lay some
seventy-five miles upstream, and from whence we fondly hoped
we were to go across the Bayuda Desert to Shendy; this idea arose
from our having been served out with maps of that route.

The orders being to start at 1.30 a.m., in order to get the
benefit of a waning moon, I was considerably pleased on being
sent ahead the previous day at a rational hour in the afternoon,
in order to buy koorbashes[1] and water-skins at a town called
Abu Gussi, thirty-five miles off. The reason was that Abu Gussi
rejoiced in a fair every Thursday, and somebody had to be sent
on in time to buy up those useful articles, of which we stood
much in need, especially the *koorbashes*.

Accordingly myself and two men started that afternoon, and
shambled ahead along a faintly visible track through the *dhurra*
fields till we lost it altogether in the darkness. Luckily I had a
compass, and the fringe of palms, occasionally visible along the
river in the distance, showed the general direction. As it got
darker, however, the compass behaved oddly; we lost sight of the
palms, and four times came to a standstill in utter bewilderment
as to our whereabouts. The only thing to be done was to inquire
the way of some inhabitant, whose fire might be yet glimmer-
ing in his shanty amongst the fields. There was some difficulty in

---

1. Cow-hide whips.

persuading those niggers we weren't going to murder them. The moment they heard our footsteps, out went their lights, and an oppressive silence reigned o'er the land; no amount of shouting and cursing of their fathers and relations would arouse them, till the magic word "baksheesh" was heard, and then out would come some impecunious native and put us back into the track for the consideration of two *piastres*. The last time we went astray we got so hopelessly lost that we concluded to bivouac under a big mimosa tree, to whose roots we tied our camels, and slept the sleep of the righteous till dawn.

The first streak of light showed us the path, of course not thirty yards off, so we pursued it in silence till about midday, when we arrived at the fair. The only incident of this journey was that, not having my eyeglass in at the time, I saw what looked like gazelles in the distance, and proceeded to stalk them. They turned out to be camels' skeletons.

A most curious and original sight the fair presented. On a gravelly slope sat multitudes of men and women, each with their basket in front of them, containing *dhurra*, cakes, butter, oil, a variety of vegetables such as *bami*, leeks, beans, and lentils, eggs, cucumbers, cotton goods, both neat and gaudy (from Manchester), bread, string, sheepskins, and cheese, but no *koorbashes* or water-skins The babble of tongues was something terrific, of course chiefly proceeding from the women, whose charms were arrayed in the native dress of grease and dirty sheets. All the women were appallingly hideous, ranging from the coal-black negress to the yellow nondescript, a mixture of every race in Africa and Asia, and sometimes with a dash of Southern Europe. Every one had her hair done in the approved fashion, *viz.* parted in the middle, and hanging down in little tight plaits, ornamented with cowries and blue beads, and dripping with grease. A strong contrast to these were their lords and masters, mostly strikingly handsome men, who paraded about with great solemnity, only unbending their dignity when a bargain affected their pockets We had been considerably misled about the *koorbashes* and water-skins. The only ones visible were private property, and I had to interview their owners separately on the subject; most of these flatly refused to part with them, asking with considerable reason how on earth they were to get home without them? A few only unbent, and condescended to sell them at fabulous prices. Eventually I got some half-dozen *koorbashes* and a dozen skins for about a quarter what they asked, but that was all; I circulated the fact of my wanting these things in all the villages near, and the next day got some two dozen more, but these were nothing compared with the number we wanted.

The next thing to be done was to help buy grain for the advancing troops. Three acting Quartermasters with accompanying interpreters were already hard at work. The labour and ingenuity necessary for getting hold of the grain were immense. The natives had long ago hidden their grain in caches in their houses and fields, for fear of some marauding sheikh seizing it, and they would not be persuaded to bring it forth. Large stores were unearthed by means of threats and secret information, but the owners would not be comforted till they had the hard cash in their hands, and then their extravagant demonstrations of joy seemed to show that being paid for their goods was a most unusual thing.

The next day the rest of the brigade turned up, and encamped close by on the river. We left at 4 a.m. the morning after. Our road lay over pretty open ground, so we marched in column of companies, instead of sections of fours. On that day we got to Debbeh, an important town at the bend of the Nile. It is important as being the junction of the camel-routes along the banks of the Nile, across the desert to Khartoum, and across to El Obeid; accordingly the town is protected by a fort, garrisoned by Bashi Bazouks and a few Turkish troops, who amused themselves in the intervals of warfare by perpetrating outrages on the villages in the neighbourhood.

These men were in the service of the Mudir of Dongola, and capital troops they were. Two months before they had fought several actions with an emissary of the Mahdi's, and, although outnumbered, had defeated him utterly and eventually annihilated all his troops. During the next two days we passed over three battlefields, strewn in places with their skulls and bones.

Two days after leaving Debbeh we arrived at Ambukol, which we thought was to have been our concentrating point; it had, however, been settled to make the camp some four miles east of the town, in a district called Korti. Ambukol was formerly a place of some importance, boasting one, occasionally two kings. The town, which has a population of about a thousand, stands nearly a mile and a half off the actual river, being on a sort of narrow backwater. All the land around is wonderfully fertile, green *dhurra* fields stretching in every direction, so it made a capital country for a large force of men and camels to encamp in. On arriving at Ambukol, we were greeted with a military display by the Mudir's irregulars; they advanced on their camels in line, to the sound of tom-toms, and then halted whilst their captains displayed their horsemanship in galloping, pulling up very short, firing guns, and curvetting and prancing around *á la* riding-school master.

The show over, we wended our way to our camping ground, where we arrived in the cool of the evening, and a most delightful spot it appeared. A grove of palms along the steep banks of the river; immediately behind them fields of grass dotted with slender mimosa trees, broad patches of tall green *dhurra* and short brownish turf beyond these, changing to sand and scrub, with the faint hills of the desert in the pink distance. Such was Korti when we arrived; by the time we all left it for good, it was a good deal worse than the Long Valley at Aldershot.

CHAPTER 6

The Marines Arrive

The very next morning (the 15th December), Lord Wolseley arrived in the Mudir's steamer from Dongola, and approved of the site selected for the camp. Till the big tents arrived from downstream, we put up shelters as best we might, improvising them with blankets, bushes, waterproof sheets, rifles, and trees.

Although the heat was still considerable, I don't remember it ever at that time rising above 100°, even at midday; as long as the blessed north wind kept blowing, the weather was very pleasant, much cooler than it had been down the river. By the way, this north wind is a providential natural institution; the heated air from Central Africa naturally rising, cool air rushes south from Europe to take its place, and the consequence is a strong, pleasant north wind for most of the year, which to a considerable extent counteracts the great natural heat. Besides reducing the temperature, it was most useful in helping the whaler-boats of the Expedition upstream; with both lugsails set, a boat used sometimes to make as much as twenty-five miles a day against the current.

For the next week or more, our time was chiefly occupied with brigade field-days, on camel-back, with the Mounted Infantry. The drill was as previously described, which we brought to a fair state of perfection: the quickest time on record, from the word of command, "Close order," to "Prepare for Cavalry," being just one minute twenty seconds. The brigade part of the drill was done by the battalion camel-masses and defending squares flanking each other in echelon, and other manoeuvres the same as Infantry Brigade Drill. The location of these field-days was the desert, about a mile off the river, where it was hard gravel or sand, and first-rate going.

The ground we passed over mostly was covered with large pebbles of all sorts, sizes, and colours; agates, crystals, garnets, and blood-stones were there in hundreds. Alas! we knew not their value. One of our men (Woods) used to walk out every afternoon, and come back with a large assortment of what he called diamonds and rubies. We only laughed at him, and called him a fool for his pains; but long afterwards he decidedly got the laugh of us. On returning to Alexandria with his diamonds he offered one to a jeweller, who gave him £16 for it! He would have made a lot of money if he had sold them all to this man, but preferred trying to sell them in London. The jeweller he went to there, however, informed him they were not of the first water, and were only saleable abroad, where they were made up into third-rate diamond ornaments which would not be looked at in England.

To return. Besides these field-days in the early morning, there was "stable" duty three times a day. I maintain now, as I maintained then, that a camel need not and ought not to be groomed like a horse. By all means get the camel-lines clean, and in as good order as is possible; give them their forage at stated times, and doctor their sore backs; but a camel is not by nature intended to be groomed, so do not groom him. The natives never do it, and the animal himself strongly objects to the process; you might as well groom an Irish pig. With infinite pains you beat the dust out of his skin, remove as many as you can of the ticks and maggots that infest him, wipe his nose (if he has a cold), and finish up by washing off any mud, and drying him with a wisp of *dhurra* stalk. What is the result? The moment your back is turned over he goes, and enjoys a delicious roll in the dust and dirt again, making himself filthier than before. The natives understand this, and. instead of cleaning him, and making him thus more susceptible to the heat of the sun, plaster him all over with mud during the hot months, which keeps the sun and flies off during the day, and, maybe, protects him somewhat from the cold at night.

INGRATITUDE.

Every day arrived driblets of troops: part of the Sussex (35th), Duke of Cornwall's Light Infantry (46th), Essex (56th), Gordon Highlanders (75th), Black Watch (42nd), and Staffordshire (38th) in whalers; Commissariat, Transport, Hospital, and Engineers' stores on *nuggers*; some companies of Heavies and Lights, on their camels; another squadron of the 19th Hussars, and, on the 26th, four officers and 101 men of the Marines, come to be attached to us as our 4th company.

Of our seven detachments, three (Grenadiers) formed the 1st company, two (Scots Guards) the 2nd, and two (Coldstream) the 3rd; the Marines now came to make up the 4th company of the Guards' Camel Regiment. They had been at Suakin for the last six months, and were originally to be brought up the Nile to form Lord Wolseley's bodyguard; that idea, however, was soon changed, so they were supplied with camels and sent to make up our regiment as aforesaid.

Excessively smart they looked, as they came into camp and formed up correctly on their markers. They were in the same uniform as ourselves, but their helmets were snow-white (ours had been stained coffee-colour), and their belts and pouches had been freshly pipe-clayed (ours were brown leather). Their grey tunics were spotless, and so were their breeches; in fact, they looked as if they had been turned out of a bandbox only the day before, yet their tunics dated from Suakin, and their

44

breeches, etc. from Wady Halfa. Their movements also equalled their appearance.

All this time, reports were rife as to where we were going to: whether up the river, to punish the devils who killed poor Colonel Stewart, or across the desert to Shendy. News had come in of Gordon's still successful defence of Khartoum. Major Kitchener's spies told how the Mahdi had written to Gordon, beseeching him not to waste more lives and time, but to deliver up the city to himself, the "divine worker of miracles"; how Gordon had replied that if he could work miracles, he had better swim his army across, and take the town; how the Mahdi had accordingly collected his army, chanted some spells, and sent them all into the river, with the result that two hundred fanatics were drowned, and the rest paddled back half-dead; how, in consequence, the Mahdi's prestige had declined, and he was residing in a hole underground in fear of his life; how his Emirs had bade him lead them and their men in an assault, since his life was so charmed that no infidel bullet could touch him; how he had refused to risk his valuable self; how his army was perishing from want of food; how the presence of half-a-dozen Englishmen would raise the siege; in fact, every story they (the spies) thought would be acceptable to us, whether true or not.

The great difficulty the Intelligence Department had to contend against was, of course, the untrustworthiness of news from all parts. The natural bent of a native's mind, when asked for news, is, without any reference whatever to the real truth, to state what he thinks would be most acceptable to his hearers, i.e. if they are in a position to reward him. Added to this the difficulty, if not danger, of communication across the desert, and the extreme reluctance of any friendly native to traverse it, you have some idea of the obstacles thrown in the way of getting at news, vitally important though it might be to the success of the whole expedition. News might come from several quarters: across the Bayuda from Metemmeh, from Khartoum direct, down the river from Berber, or even *via* Berber, Abu Hamed, Korosko, and telegraphed up again, yet look at the time it would take, the distances from Khartoum being respectively 276, 210, 515, and 660 miles. The Mahdi also used to send emissaries across to us, purporting to be friends, whereas they invariably gave false information, stating that there was no enemy at all between us and Khartoum, that the Mahdi's forces were deserting in large numbers, etc. etc.—anything to mislead us as to his real intentions. No wonder then that news reached us but seldom, and that still more seldom was it trustworthy.

In order to test the steadiness of our camels as regarded noise and firing, the 19th Hussars one day, at brigade drill, charged down on the unprotected mass of camels, cheering and yelling. Everybody expected to see them break their ropes, and career wildly over the desert. The only result was that one solitary camel struggled to his feet, looked round, and knelt down again; the others never moved an eyelid. That was satisfactory; and as firing into them with blank cartridge, and over them with ball, had already been tried at Shabadud with no visible results, the general opinion was that they would stand charging niggers or anything else in creation with equanimity. Sad to say, we came to the conclusion that it was want of brains, *pur et simple*, that caused our steeds to behave thus docilely; any other animal with a vestige of mind would have been scared to death, but, as it was, no one regretted their deficiency.

Another way of occupying spare time was going on outpost duty at night in the scrub, half-a-mile out of camp. Barring the difficulty of finding your picquet and detached posts in the bushes when you had started to go the rounds, it was simple work. One distinguished officer of the G.C.R., however, found it anything but simple, for, owing to a dearth of officers of his rank, he had to superintend the outposts for six or seven days running; he was in a deplorable state at the end, and went for ever afterwards by the name of "the Field Officer."

On Christmas Eve occurred the first casualty in the G.C.R. A private of the Scots Guards (Tomlinson) died of enteric fever, and was buried with full honours next day. Sir Herbert Stewart, always the best of friends to the "Brigade," gave up the flooring

of his tent to make the coffin, though there was not the smallest chance of his getting any more planks. Not many Generals
would have done that.

Christmas Day was solemnised by letting as many men off
parades and fatigues as possible, and consuming as much as we
could hold. Plum-puddings were concocted out of every imagi-
nable eatable, and eaten in due style as such. The great difficulty
lay in getting suet to make the puddings with, as the cows and
sheep of those parts do not cultivate fat. However, suet or no
suet, none of the puddings remained to tell the tale, and everybody adjourned to a concert, held on a platform between two
huge bonfires. Far from there being a want of performers, there
were but too many, and the music lasted long into the night,
when all retired to dream of home, or to gasp with the night-
marish results of the pudding.

CHAPTER 7

Abu Halfa and the Mahdists

At length on the 27th December, there was a final inspection of water-skins, necessaries, arms, kits, and accoutrements, and to our delight the report dribbled out that we were to start next day, whither we knew not. The whole of the Heavies had now arrived, and drilled with us several times, so were also ready to start. By-and-by we discovered that the Mounted Infantry had likewise received instructions to hold themselves in readiness for marching, together with a proportion of Commissariat, Hospital, Engineers, and Transport. The line regiments who had arrived by boat had not yet all made their final preparations, so we concluded that Gordon was in great difficulties, and that we were to strike across the Bayuda Desert to Metemmeh. The 38th (South Stafford) were starting in boats for Merawi on the 28th, to act as advanced guard to Earle's river column; this we knew was going upstream as soon as it possibly could, since every day caused an appreciable diminution in the waters of the Nile, and rendered the upper cataracts more difficult. Our task therefore seemed to be to take Metemmeh, hold it till the river column could get round via Abu Hamed and Berber, and then advance in force on Khartoum.

In effect, on the 28th we got our orders to start in two days.

The idea of the advance, officially communicated to us, was this: the chief necessary of a desert march being water, we were first to proceed to Gakdul wells (which lay some 100 miles into the desert), in sufficient force to overcome any resistance we should meet there, and leave a battalion (the Guards' Camel

Regiment) there to entrench itself, and hold the wells at any cost. The remainder of the force was to return to Korti for sufficient troops and transport to advance the remaining seventy-six miles to Metemmeh, and was to establish itself there, using Gakdul as an intermediate point of communication with the base at Korti.

The route from Korti, or strictly speaking from Ambukol, to Metemmeh, had very luckily been selected thirteen years previously by Ismail Pasha (then Viceroy of Egypt) for the continuation of the railway already mentioned, intended to run from Wady Halfa to Khartoum. It had been thoroughly surveyed by his engineers, under the charge of Mr. Fowler, C.E., and an accurate plan, therefore, of the 176 miles was already in our possession. This was of inestimable value to us, as, besides marking the sites of the various wells, it gave accurate information as to the quantity of water we were likely to find there. Abu Halfa and Gakdul were the largest reservoirs on the track, and as Abu Halfa was reported to have run rather dry, Gakdul was chosen as the important point for concentration.

On Tuesday, the 30th December, accordingly, the following force started from Korti: one squadron 19th Hussars, Guards' Camel Regiment, Mounted Infantry, Engineers, and an enormous camel train (1,357) bearing stores, composed of "baggagers" and the camels belonging to the Heavies and Lights, driven by natives, Aden and Somali boys, and superintended by various C.T.C. officers and N.C.Os; a proportion of the Medical Staff Corps,[1] and the Bearer Company, with camels bearing litters and *cacolets* for the sick and wounded; all under the command of Brigadier-General Sir Herbert Stewart: total, 73 officers, 1212 men and natives, and 2091 camels. Baggage we personally had none. Each man's luggage was limited to what he could carry on his camel, not exceeding 40lbs. which was amply sufficient even for the officers; it included a change of tunic, pair of boots, sponge, towel, soap, pair of socks, and a shirt; what more *could* you want? If you were extravagant enough to want a bath, a hole

---

1. Used to be the Army Medical Department, or Army Hospital Corps, but they change their name every six months.

in the sand lined with your waterproof sheet made a beautiful one; with that and one blanket rolled on the near side, and another blanket and your great-coat on the off-side, you had heaps of room in your *zuleetahs* for any amount of luxuries in the shape of French novels, sketch-books, and other articles of toilet. Half-a-dozen spare camels carried the men's cooking pots, rations, water, and our mess saucepans, and *voila tout*.

The whole force paraded on the desert plateau behind Korti at 3 p.m., and, after a quasi march past before Lord Wolseley, moved off in column of route about forty camels abreast. The track was beautiful going, and every one in high spirits at the prospect of commencing the "real business" at last. Though the spies and native informers had reported that there was no enemy at all on the route, we knew by experience that their information was not to be too much depended on, and were pretty certain that even though we might not meet with any serious resistance in the desert itself, probably we should have some fighting in getting to the river the other end. As Sir Herbert said: "I don't like unnecessary slaughter, but I'm afraid we shall have to kill five hundred or so of the poor devils before we can establish ourselves in Metemmeh." Poor fellow, he little thought of what would happen to him before he saw the Nile again.

In front of the column were half-a-dozen natives on camels, to act as guides. Sir Herbert had forced them to come in a very simple way. He had sent for the chief men at Ambukol who knew the route, sat them down in his tent, showed them many dollars, and told them they were to come as guides. They flatly refused, so the General said: "You will come anyhow. If you like a ride to Metemmeh tied on to your camels, well and good; if you prefer not being lashed on, you will get these nice presents." So they came.

They were escorted by a small party of the 19th Hussars, who had orders to shoot them down if they attempted to bolt; no such opportunity, however, occurred. The rest of the 19th preceded the whole column, scouting quite magnificently; on

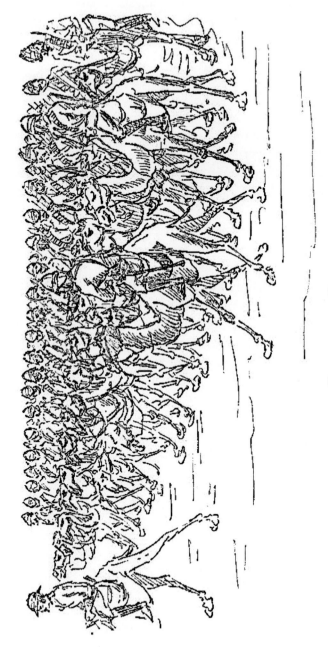

THE START FROM KORTI.

coming to a plain with hills in the distance, you'd see various specks on the tops of the furthest hills, and with the help of your glasses discover them to be the 19th. Sir Herbert was immensely pleased with them, and pointed them out to me as being the very acme of Light Cavalry.

Our first halt was only two hours after we started, the object being to give the men their tea, since we were going to march all night. Fires were easily kindled with the dry grass and mimosa bushes which abounded along the track, and the tea having been consumed (very good it was, too), we started ahead again, the darkness being illuminated by a three-quarter full moon.

I had had a vague idea, before starting from England, that it was perpetual summer in the tropics both as regards heat and light, but discovered before long that the sun rises and sets in Africa at more or less the same time as in colder climates, and, this being December, it sank below the horizon at about five o'clock. Luckily for us, the moon appeared shortly after the sun set, and we plodded on all night in a beautiful white light, much stronger than I ever saw in England. I had to make a road-report, and, thanks to the moon, could see every black hill in the distance clearly enough to take a bearing on.

It was a novel and pleasant sensation going ahead of the column in the quiet moonlit desert, not a sound being made by the two thousand camels in rear as their padded feet passed over the sand. By-and-by the men got sleepy, and their laughter and talking grew fainter and fainter, till at last it ceased altogether. I got desperately sleepy myself, and beastly cold, altogether not in a very fit state for surveying; however, I kept awake by a great effort, and took copious notes to keep warm. Ever and again came a faint bugle sound from the rear, intimating that the baggagers were lagging; the sound was passed on from bugler to bugler, and the order given to halt the column till the rearguard came up.

Sometimes when several camels' loads had slipped and the rear-guard halted till they were fixed again, the halt would last twelve or fifteen minutes; so in that case I made a note of the exact hour, slipped off my camel, and went fast asleep till the "advance" woke me up again. I thus timed every halt accurately, the only way it was possible to check the distance gone, allowing exactly two and three-quarter miles for every sixty minutes on the go. This measurement, I found, answered wonderfully well, for on arrival at Gakdul I was within two miles of the distance given on Fowler's map. A camel kindly paces exactly one yard, though you would have thought his long legs would cover much more. In going faster or slower than his ordinary pace, he only increases or diminishes the number of paces per minute, and not the length of his stride, which is also very obliging of him. In fact, every camel is an accurate walking pedometer, and a first-rate animal for surveying the country from. Potiphar was no exception; the only thing that annoyed me was that he never would stand still to let me get an exact bearing; just as the needle of the compass was getting steady, round he whisked, and so did the needle. I believe he did it on purpose.

I must not forget to mention here the smallest, but by no means the least important member of the expedition, namely Jacky. Jacky was a little dog of unknown breed, something between a King Charles spaniel and a Dandie Dinmont. The only thing certain about his parentage was that he was English, for he had strongly resented any attempts at familiarity on the part of the pariahs or other foreign dogs, and had attached himself at once to one of our companies at Assouan. He had tramped the whole way from Assouan to Korti, and now he was coming with us to Khartoum if possible. Though his body was small, Jacky's heart was big for, besides being an affectionate little dog, he refused to be carried on a camel even when tired, and trotted along with his nose in the air, disdaining all offers of help. He went through most of the fighting afterwards, and came back with us to Korti, where I eventually lost sight of him. Let us hope he returned to his native shores in safety.

The country we were passing over was still hard sand or gravel, with low ranges of pitch-black hills rising all over the place. Most curious shapes they were, often exactly like a beefsteak pudding, varying from that to a plum-cake; round smooth hills emerging in many cases from an expanse of bare sand, and seldom connected together. Where the tracks led close to any of these hills, there were scrubby mimosa shrubs, and long yellow grass; in more favoured parts the mimosa trees rose to a height of ten or twelve feet, showing there must be subsoil water nearly throughout the desert.

Day broke towards five o'clock, and at six the reveille bugle was received with ironical cheers. About an hour and a half afterwards we crossed a hard, cracked mud plain, up a slope into a *khor*, between two ranges of hills. As trees abounded, though no water was visible, we halted at 8.30, posted a few vedettes and sentries, and after a hearty breakfast went fast asleep till the midday heat and flies woke us up again.

How flies and insects of sorts manage to exist in the Desert was always a puzzle to me. I always imagined that insects required a certain amount of dampness, but no the common or garden fly was as much at home on the driest slopes of the Bayuda Desert as in a lodging-house kitchen in England. Curious insects crawled about the yellow grass, the exact facsimile of the blades; unless you saw them moving on their cranky swaying legs, you would never imagine them to be other than dry sticks or blades of grass. A merciful dispensation of Providence has ordained that no mosquitoes, bugs, or fleas should live south of Wady Halfa, so the only annoying insects were common flies and sand-flies, which latter only flourish on the banks of the river.

At 3 p.m. we started again, and proceeded in much the same order, with an hour's interval for tea, till 8.30, when we arrived at the first wells, Abu Hashim or Hambok by name. They were simply funnel-shaped holes in the grass, from four to twelve feet deep, with hardly any water in them at all. Accordingly we pushed on for the next wells, El Howeiyat, some thirteen miles further. The ground now got somewhat steeper, and at midnight we emerged on a broad stony *khor*.

As soon as it became known that we had entered on the

New Year, the whole column struck up *Auld Lang Syne*, and the echoes of the chorus in the surrounding hills produced a rare effect; not often, I should think, have those rocks heard that sort of music. After *Auld Lang Syne*, songs of all sorts were started, and by the time everyone had shouted themselves hoarse with the choruses we had arrived at the wells of El Howeiyat. These were very similar to the holes at Hambok, though slightly better filled with the necessary fluid. A halt was therefore ordered and the horses of the 19th given a bucketful apiece. Long before they were satisfied, the wells were dry, and the rest of the column fast asleep.

At six the reveille was sounded, and the force was soon on the move again. At midday we debouched into a vast scrub-covered plain, intersected by myriads of tiny dry watercourses and bounded on the left by the Gebel Gilif range. Just as we halted for the midday meal, a Hussar appeared, dragging a stalwart native after him, whom he had found hiding in the long grass. This turned out to be no other than Abu Loolah, a famous robber who had been the terror of passing caravans. The guides gathered round him, chattering all at once, and demanded his instant decapitation. Though seemingly in the presence of an unlimited amount of enemies, Abu Loolah did not lose his stolidity, putting it no doubt all down to *Kismet*. Sir Herbert, however, considered him far too valuable to lose in this way, so made him accompany us as an extra guide, the other natives keeping at a respectful distance from him. Ten minutes afterwards another Hussar brought in his wife, a decidedly handsome young woman, with barely a stitch of clothing to cover her charms; she had likewise been caught after a long chase, in which she very nearly gave her captor the slip. A small party was then sent to their shanty to bring in their household goods, consisting of a camel, a baby, some wooden bowls, corn, and a kid. Thus the family travelled with us, the whole perched on top of their unfortunate camel.

After a rest of three hours we moved on again, intending to get to Gakdul by next morning at daybreak. About midnight the whole column was halted, to allow the indefatigable 19th to

ABU LOOLAH AND FAMILY.

find out the reason of a faint light burning far off on the plains. After half-an-hour's absence they returned with several natives, a string of camels, and several loads of dates. They had found a number of natives and camels bivouacked for the night, surprised them, captured as much loot as possible, and bolted the rest. The caravan turned out to be one loaded with stores from the Lower Nile for the Mahdi's troops; the provisions consisted chiefly of dates, so what the Hussars could not carry away they carefully pitched into holes, and strewed about in the grass.

At 3.15 a.m. we crossed the track leading to the Abu Halfa wells, which lay three or four miles N.E. of our route. A party of Mounted Infantry was accordingly sent thither to explore, whilst the rest of the column pushed on to Gakdul. The Mounted Infantry found some twenty men in the Mahdi's uniform[2] round the wells, took four prisoners, and bolted the rest. The prisoners lost their temper, tore off their uniform, and spat on it. This ebullition of feeling was taken for what it was worth, and they were sent on to Gakdul in their native nakedness, whilst the party of Mounted Infantry entrenched themselves at the wells.

---

2. This uniform was simply a long white night-shirt, covered with scraps of blue and red cloth, and a coloured straw skull-cap; the higher the rank, the more decorated they were.

CHAPTER 8

Building Forts

About seven o'clock, we turned imperceptibly into the track leading to the wells. So imperceptible was the difference in direction, that at first I could not make out why the sun pursued such a curiously crooked course. Suddenly it dawned on me that we ought to be close on the wells, according to calculation, and that the track was making a very gradual bend to the east.

The way now began to get very unpleasant, the ground being strewn with large round stones, which made the camels slither about in a dangerous way, and seriously disturbed the dressing of the column. We were now entering a sort of broad defile, hemmed in apparently on all sides by steep, rocky, black hills. The column now halted for ten minutes to allow the rear to close up, and for the 19th to find out whether the wells were in possession of the enemy. The Hussars speedily climbed their ponies up the hills, found the place deserted, posted vedettes on the highest rocks, and sent back to report. The column accordingly advanced through a narrow pass, barely one hundred yards wide, into a tiny plain, culminating in a regular *cul-de-sac*. "Where, oh, where are the wells?" inquired everybody. They were not to be seen at first, till the Intelligence Department, in the shape of Major Kitchener, pointed out a steep wall of rock at the far end. On peeping round this, we discovered a magnificent pool of water, about twenty yards by thirty, and apparently of unknown depth, for the rocks went perpendicularly down into it.

The column formed up gingerly on the nubbly stones, dismounted with difficulty, as the camels objected to kneeling on such unpleasant ground, and proceeded to unload stores, etc. I concluded to explore the wells thoroughly, so tied Potiphar to a tree, and arduously climbed to the top of the precipice overhanging the aforesaid pool. There were said to be two more pools above the lower one, communicating with each other, and these were easily found; that is to say, I saw down into them from above, but did not see how to get at them, since they lay at the bottom of the usual perpendicular rocks. However, after much difficulty and sliding about, I got down to the upper one; even then the water lay so far below me, I could hardly dip my cup into it, but when I did reach it the drink was over and above sufficient reward for the climb. The middle pool had now to be reached by a steep sort of narrow channel through the rock. I shoved myself in, legs foremost, and immediately slid down about ten yards, being only brought up short by clinging to the rock on either side. The bed of the channel was as slippery as ice, owing to the friction from the torrents that pour through during the rainy season, and the passage itself terminated abruptly five feet above the pool. By dint of digging my toes into a crack or two, I succeeded in standing up in comfort. What a beautiful sight it was! Eighty feet above my head towered an overhanging precipice of black rock; behind me rose another of the same height; at the foot of the one in front lay a beautiful, large, ice-green pool, deepening into black as I looked into its transparent depths. Scarlet dragon-flies flitted about in the shade; rocks covered with dark-green weed looked out of the water; the air was cool almost to coldness. It was like being dropped into a fairy grotto, at least so it seemed to me after grilling for days in the sun.

I drank as much of the water as I could conveniently hold, filled my water-bottle as a specimen for the thirsty souls below, and went to the lower end of this beautiful pool, where a similar channel connected it with the lowest of all. I climbed into it, and found myself overlooking the large pool about twelve feet below, where rows of horses and camels were drinking at the far end. As this pool was notoriously only fit for animals, stray Arabs watering their flocks and camels there, and washing their beastly selves in it, my first thought was naturally how the cool water of the upper pools was to be brought to the men, since they apparently could not reach it without much difficulty. The obvious way seemed to be to lead it through the channels, but how was the fresh water to pass the dirty water through it, above it, or how? It could not go round it, for the cliffs were perpendicular. The General's foresight had provided for this, and on returning below, I found the Engineers had, in addition to half-a-dozen small pumps, brought nearly one hundred yards of hose, amply sufficient to reach the upper wells. I wanted the hose to lie along inflated water-skins, on the pool, but my suggestion was pooh-poohed, and the hose suffered to lie along the bottom; I predicted it would rot in the water, but it didn't.

The water supply being thus assured, and amply sufficient (the upper pools containing each more than half the contents of the camel-pool), the next thing to be done was to hold the wells. The Engineers were to stay with the Guards' Camel Regiment, whilst the others went back for more troops and stores, so they were at once told off to help plan two forts, one at the entrance to the cul-de-sac, the other immediately above the wells.

By the midday meal, all stores had been unloaded, and piled in a glen close to the wells, "covered" by the future fort. During the afternoon, most of us indulged in the first wash we had had since leaving Korti, whilst others not so cleanly inclined sought to sleep awhile. At dusk, having given all the beasts a good drink, the returning force "fell in," with all the available camels; they even took away all our steeds, for baggage purposes, only kindly leaving us some half-dozen who were too sick to go back. By eight o'clock the column had disappeared, leaving us alone in our glory with 6 Hussars, 15 Engineers, and a vast store of Commissariat to keep us company.

The returning force only intended to clear out of the defile, and pass the night immediately outside on the plain before beginning their journey. It was about time to get a little sleep, as we had been going for eighty-four hours without more than four hours' consecutive sleep. The distance traversed, not quite one hundred miles according to Fowler, had been done in sixty-four hours, thirty-four hours on the move and thirty broken up into short halts; the rate of travelling was therefore just under three miles an hour call it two and three-quarter miles, taking the average rate of camels at that; this result always turned out fairly accurate.

Allowing Sir Herbert's baggage train half as much time again to get comfortably to Korti, the same back to Gakdul, and forty-eight hours to collect troops and stores at Korti, we considered that we ought to see them back in ten days at the outside, and then, hooray for the advance! There was plenty to be done before they came back: forts to build, roads to make, camps, etc. to mark out, and reconnoitring to be done.

The men were told off in fatigues for the various duties, and splendidly they worked; their shoe-leather never recovered it. Smooth roads were formed all about the enclosure by picking up the objectionable stones, and paths hacked in the rocks to the various points of interest, such as the forts and picquet stations. The forts rose slowly, inch by inch, and I venture to say that if the workmen had been any others than Guardsmen and Marines, the walls would never have risen so quickly from the ground. As it was, the walls in ten days rose to over five feet high, a marvellous piece of work considering the few men we had, the size of the forts, and the enormous difficulty there was in getting material. All the loose stones in the neighbourhood were collected and built into the walls; that occupied four days; for the remainder of the time every stone had to be loosened out of the solid rock with pickaxes and worked with levers, till it could be carried to its proper place. Considering that there were only three pickaxes and two crowbars for each fort, the one measuring roughly 20 yards by 23, the other 30 yards by 15, the amount of work done was something extraordinary.

Outpost duty was rather severe, especially at night. Since we were by no means sure that the enemy might not be meditating a night attack on our *cul-de-sac*, we had to keep many sentries go-

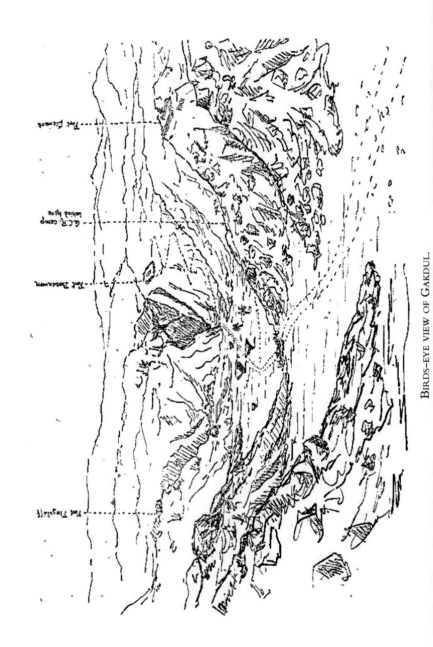

Fort Sitearock

Q.C.R. camp
behind here

Fort Baccarawen

Fort Flagstaff

BIRDS-EYE VIEW OF GAKDUL.

ing. Two officers and some sixty-five men were on outpost duty every twenty-four hours. Since several high hills commanded all the tracks, ravines, and gullies by which we might be attacked, it was easy enough to post sentries during the day to see for many miles round. At night, however, it was different; a chain of sentries had to be established round the whole place, and with so many glens and gullies it was impossible to command the whole satisfactorily with a few men on a pitch-dark night. Oh, the agony of going the rounds four or five times a night! The whole distance on a map would not exceed three-quarters of a mile, if as much, but the fastest time on record was forty-eight minutes for the whole round. Uphill and downhill, over those sharp rocks, no path visible, as your lantern would infallibly go out at the first cropper, skinning your shins over every big stone, climbing down precipices you would never attempt by daylight, losing your way, your hat, your bearings. On these black nights, any enterprising nigger could have "croaked" a sentry; the wonder was that it didn't happen. The wear and tear to shoe-leather was something awful; not one of us had a decent pair of boots at the end of the first week.

Occasionally during the day, an officer or sentry on outpost would spot a native, miles off in the plain, and signal it down to the C.O. The Intelligence Department, still happily represented by Major Kitchener, V——, D——, and some Hussars, would promptly saddle any beasts that came to hand, and scoot out after him. Several times the reconnaissance party captured and scattered a caravan bringing dates and stores for the Mahdi, and we soon had quite a respectable amount of prisoners. On one occasion an unfortunate native who was overtaken offered a Medjidie dollar, his little all, to Kitchener as a ransom! News was also communicated from outside the valley by a heliograph, which signalled any unusual occurrence in any direction; in fact, the only direction from which an unexpected enemy might arrive was that above the wells, towards the heart of the mountain-range.

Being certain that there ought to be more water some-

GOING THE ROUNDS AT NIGHT (GAKDUL).

where in the hills, N—— and I one day followed up the torrent track above the wells. The scene in the rainy reason must
be grand beyond description. The smooth round boulders, the
uprooted mimosa trees, the occasional pot-holes in the rock,
and the general aspect of the torrent bed, all bore witness to
the destructive violence of the masses of water that tear down
from the hills on to the plain below every summer. The natives
report that on the vast gravelly plain of the Bayuda the rain-
water reaches for a few days the depth of over two feet, but is
quickly sucked up by the thirsty sand. If that is so down below,
what must be the scene in the hills when the rains are in full
swing! I should like to see it, from a balloon.

We climbed and struggled over the boulders for some time
without finding any water, till we were brought up short by seeing some greenish liquid oozing out from under a rock. It was
discovered to be a spring, but the water was warm and slimy,

and probably unwholesome. A short distance off was another similar one, likewise nasty, so we did not pull up till we came to a pot-hole in the rock, about six feet across, and ten deep, half full of beautifully clear water. Having forgotten to bring a cup, and our water-bottles being too light to sink by themselves, we tied a baccy bag to a stick and drank in comfort. During the manoeuvres employed to fill the bag with water, my precious pipe fell out of my pocket into the hole. I couldn't reach so far with my arm, and our extemporised cup was too small to fish it out with, so we employed the last resource: N—— held me by the heels, whilst I slid down the perpendicular side and fished it out. Of course, whilst I was being hauled up in this inverted position, most of the other things fell out of my pockets, and I had to go down again. One tiny tin of meat lozenges is there to this day, but the other articles, being floatable, were recovered.

We then pursued our way till we got to a stony little plain, with faint gazelle and jackal tracks, all converging in one direction, which could only mean one thing water. In fact, after a few minutes' walk, we suddenly came upon an immense pool of rain-water, similar to those below, and hemmed in on all sides by steep rocks. I had luckily a quantity of string in my pocket, so as we wanted to gauge the contents of the reservoir, I stripped and plunged in. Owing to the shape of the thing, I could not take a header into deep water, and the cold of the water driving the blood to my head made me turn dizzy and nearly faint; however, ducking my head made me feel better at once. Having previously tied a stone to the end of my string, I let it slip when about half-way across; to my surprise it kept quite taut right to the end, twenty-four feet of it. That was deep enough for anybody, so after a delicious swim in the cool water, I got out, and the sun dried me in less than half-a-minute. The pool we calculated to be about twenty yards by twelve, with an average depth of at least eighteen feet big enough to last a big force some time. A shout from N—— now announced he had discovered another one higher up the rocks, situated immediately above the big pool, and about half its size. So far, so good; if the Gakdul wells gave out, we might depend on this as a last extremity, but the question how we were to get the camels up, or the water down to the plain, we left to a future occasion: as it happened, these reserve wells were never used. We fully intended to go there some night and wait for gazelle, but, somehow, never did; we had enough nights out of bed as it was.

Sometimes, when on outpost during the day, a sentry would (according to orders) report a gazelle in the distance, and any officer within hail would proceed to stalk it, but hardly any were got this way; they were fearfully shy beasts, and the ground was rather too broken for a comfortable stalk. You would mark down one behind a rock, but by the time you had worked your way up behind him, he wasn't there.

A third fort, a tiny one on an outstanding ridge flanking the wells and the other two works, was now constructed and finished in a couple of days, and a road hacked up to it. By the time Sir Herbert arrived, we flattered ourselves he would not know the place again.

CHAPTER 9

Advance of the Column

On the 11th of January a convoy arrived under Colonel Stanley Clarke, consisting of stores and ammunition. Luckily, I happened to be on outpost that night, and escaped the fiendish clatter and noise that his 1,000 camels made in getting to the wells to drink native drivers jabbering, camels bellowing, Englishmen swearing all night through. By an elaborate arrangement of pumps, hose, and troughs, the Engineers had contrived to allow thirty camels to water at a time (the original entrance only allowing three or four); yet watering 1,000 camels took a considerable time far into the night and dawn was breaking by the time they had all finished. Next day the fighting part of the force arrived, under Sir Herbert, and with great joy did we welcome back our steeds, who were already showing signs of short rations and hard work; their humps were diminishing, the saddles working loose, and sore backs ensued. Our camels brought back some 400 of the 35th (Sussex) Regiment, who were to garrison the wells, under their Colonel, Vandeleur, whilst we went ahead.

Orders were issued by the General to start the next day but one; accordingly the intervening day was employed in watering the whole force again, seeing to the arms and ammunition (170 rounds a man), and issuing stores.

As much water as possible was taken in iron camel-tanks, two to a camel, but the condition of our private water-skins and leather bottles was pitiable. Every man had been served out afresh with both skin and bottle on starting from Korti, and yet barely twenty per cent, of the skins held their full complement of water. Even after every visible hole had been carefully sewn up, and the whole skin thoroughly greased, at the end of the first day's march you would find more than half your water evaporated; next day the skin would be a damp, flabby bag, and the day after a dried, shrivelled-up article without an atom of water in it. How a committee of intelligent officers can ever have selected such an article beats my comprehension! The long Egyptian leathern water-bottles (*musseks*) were even worse, letting the water out in streams through the seams. The orders about water were that every man was to replenish his little wooden English bottle from the *mussek* for his private use, and on no account to touch his skin, which was to be used for public purposes, such as making tea and cooking fresh meat. However, when his wooden bottle, holding one pint, was exhausted, and the water in his *mussek* had evaporated, what was he to do? We made a few men sew up their waterproof sheets into water-bags, but thorns and sharp stones had played havoc with the water-tightness of most of them. The sailors were better off, for they had brought up a quantity of large India-rubber bags, specially made for the purpose. I wish the Government would have gone to the expense of providing every one with them; it would have saved an enormous amount of pain and privation.

On Wednesday, the 13th of January, the new column paraded outside the hills on the plain, and at 2 p.m. we moved off in columns of companies, Heavies leading, ourselves next, baggage and stores in the centre, and Mounted Infantry to bring up the rear. The actual numbers were:

Division, Naval Brigade, with one Gardner gun	about 30 of all ranks
Heavy Camel Regiment	about 380 of all ranks
Three troops, 19th Hussars	about 90 of all ranks
Half Battery, Royal Artillery, with three 7-pounder screw guns	about 30 of all ranks
Royal Engineers	about 25 of all ranks
Guards' Camel Regiment	about 367 of all ranks
Mounted Infantry Regiment	about 360 of all ranks
Sussex	about 100 of all ranks

Medical and Commissariat Staff   about 45 of all ranks
Native drivers   about 120 of all ranks
Total (roughly speaking), about 1500 men, 90 horses, and 2200 camels

The Hussars were, of course, mounted on their own horses, little wiry grey Egyptian stallions, hardly deserving the name of horses. I should properly call them ponies, as not one reached fifteen hands; little beasts always full of go, whether they got their rations or not, having a capacity for going without water for an extraordinary length of time; no English horse could have gone through the time they had during the next week with any chance of life; yet they seemed to thrive on desert air and crumbly dry grass. All the rest of the force (with the exception of the natives, who walked) were mounted on camels gunners, blue-jackets and all. I forgot to mention that Colonel Burnaby arrived with a convoy of grain, just in time to come on with us, but the grain was mostly left at Gakdul and the camels impressed for carrying stores and rations. Only sufficient corn was brought on to allow of two feeds per camel of eight pounds each; the fact was that the authorities had stopped buying camels on the Nile, and two camels were made to do the work of three; consequently there were not enough to carry grain for the force, and the camels had to sustain themselves on mimosa shoots and long, dry yellow grass, a hundredweight of which would barely produce a pound of nourishment. The Naval Division under Lord C. Beresford, Lieutenants Piggott, Munro, and De Lisle, brought one Gardner gun with them, but were only allowed 1000 rounds of ammunition. Considering that the gun[1] fired over 100 rounds a minute, this was only allowing it ten minutes' work at the outside more false economy.

The three guns brought by the Artillery were 7lb. screw guns (i.e. made to screw together), three powerful camels carrying one gun and ammunition between them; 100 rounds per gun were brought.

The next four divisions have been already described: it only remains for me to say a word about the Medical, Bearer Com-

1. The identical ill-fated one that jammed at Tamai.

pany, Commissariat, and Transport arrangements. Besides the camels carrying stretchers and medical stores, and the doctors superintending them, a large quantity of camels had been fitted for the reception of sick and wounded, with litters and *cacolets*. These were in charge of a section of the Bearer Company, an off-shoot of the Medical Staff during war time, and most useful they proved. The Commissariat was in immediate charge of Deputy Commissary Nugent, C.B., an invaluable man, with a head like a calculating-machine. His train consisted of about 800 camels, carrying stores of all sorts, and driven by Aden boys, negroes, and natives of all sorts, clothed in a red turban, a blue jersey, a haversack, and a brass ticket nothing more. The reason for such a large quantity of stores was that it was intended to form a large depot at Metemmeh before advancing on Khartoum; and this was the first instalment—provisions for 1500 men for a month.

Chapter 10

The Enemy in Sight

The first afternoon's going was over a vast gravelly plain, with gentle undulations. As we pursued our way S.E., the Gebel Gilif range faded away in the distance towards the East, and when we halted for the night at 6 o'clock, the hills were almost invisible.

Our resting-place was a hard, sandy slope, dotted here and there with tussocks of dry grass and mimosa bushes, which were speedily utilised for fuel. Every one of the baggage camels had to be unloaded, as they could not rest comfortably with their loads on, and by the time they had been fed it was quite dark.

Sentries were posted at some distance off on each flank of the resting column, in order to give the alarm in plenty of time if the enemy should appear, and try to rush us. The column was so halted that in case of attack the different regiments could quickly form square at any angle of the camels, and flank each other and the vast mass of baggagers and stores.

Reveille woke us at next morning at 3 a.m., and by 4.30 we had had our breakfasts and were on the move. It is very cold in the early morning in the desert, especially during January, and the comfort of a steaming cup of cocoa or tea, with biscuit and cold bully beef, must be felt to be appreciated. Although I own bully is not inviting at midday, when floating about the tin in red, warm, stringy masses, yet it has its period of beauty, in the early mornings, when the cold night has solidified it into respectable-looking cold beef; at that time a quarter of a pound of it inside you, washed down with hot drink, makes a deal of difference in the way you are disposed to look at things on a dark and cold morning.

Shortly after day broke, we saw the Gebel en Nus in the distance. It is a well-known landmark in the Bayuda, being a tall conical hill sticking straight up out of the sand, and visible for many miles round. My company, worse luck, was detailed for baggage guard that morning: this irksome duty consisted in keeping a short way behind the baggage train, and whacking up any camel or driver who lagged behind. Every five minutes a load would slip off, or a camel fall down sick; in that case a couple of men were at once detailed to dismount, help load up the camel, and whack it along again. As all the baggagers were in strings of three, tied nose to tail, each string in charge of one native driver, the downfall of one meant the stoppage of the three; the other two camels generally did not comprehend why they should stop, and hauled away till their head-gear or tail-ropes gave way, or else got themselves so entangled with each other that their loads dropped off, and then the whole thing had to be done again; it was an endless business, and provocative of much swearing. Generally by the time the three camels were reloaded and set going again, the column was nearly out of sight, with nothing behind but the rear-guard, who had strict orders not to allow any one behind them.

We had not gone far on this morning, when there was a violent commotion just in front of me amongst the baggage train, and an enormous riderless camel appeared tearing its way through the others. It charged my company, and threw it into some confusion; no one could catch hold of it, as it had no headgear to hang on by, and it was still cantering awkwardly about my ranks, when its rider appeared in the shape of W——, somewhat out of breath from pursuing his steed through the sand, but trying to look as if he liked it. It seemed that his camel, a brute noted for its evil habits, had managed somehow to slip its bridle off, and on finding itself free had indulged in a series of violent kicks. W—— stuck on like a monkey, but when the brute proceeded to bolt, and there was nothing to guide it by, he thought it was time to get off, and did so speedily, arriving on his head in the soft sand. His camel was at length lassoed and remounted, and W—— trotted off to his place none the worse.

AN ANNOYING TRICK.

Soon after this little episode, the track (or rather where the track ought to have been) led over some very soft sand-hills, rather a feature at this particular place. The wind coming from the north drives mounds of fine drift sand before it, which advance very slowly, but with an irresistible force, overwhelming landmarks, rocks, and trees, and only to be stopped by running water (of which there isn't any). It is a terrible place for losing one's way, since these sand-hills extend for over half-a-mile, and entirely obliterate the track. This is especially unpleasant on the return journey, as there are no hills or landmarks visible anywhere. Several camels went head over heels down the soft slopes, and lay there with their legs in the air, unable to right themselves with their loads on.

At ten o'clock we halted for the midday meal, and rested two hours. Just as we were going to start again, the rear-guard (Scots Guards Company) turned up, having had tremendous work driving up stragglers and reloading broken-down camels. If a camel dropped in his tracks, his load and saddle were taken off him and loaded on another (already loaded) camel. The few spare camels had been used up long ago, so the stores had to be packed at any cost on animals already weakened by fatigue and short rations. The way the poor brutes toiled on was something marvellous; you would see one go slower and slower, till the tail of the animal in front he was tied to seemed nearly coming off; then he would stop for a second, give a mighty shiver, and drop down stone-dead. If he fell alive, but could not go on, he was left there. It sounds cruel not to have shot them at once, but the majority of those thus left rested for some time, then staggered up to browse on the dry grass and mimosa trees, and thus prolonged their life some days. A great many recovered sufficiently to travel to various small wells, guided by their marvellous instinct for finding water; in fact, at one well (El Faar), a long time afterwards, no fewer than seventy-three camels were found, in the last stage of thinness and sore backs of course, but very much alive all the same!

The column passed Gebel en Nus at one o'clock, and forthwith the scenery changed. We now entered a broad valley, covered with grass and really decent sized trees, some as much as twenty feet high—still no water visible, though I have no doubt there was plenty close under the surface. All round were rocky hills, sometimes forming low ridges across the track, sometimes receding into the distance; far away ahead could be seen the Gebel es Sergain (Hill of the Saddle), which had been previously selected as our halting-place for the night.

At five o'clock we reached it. The ground was cut up into sandy water-channels, making most comfortable sleeping ground, but very unpleasant for any one to I get over at night. Accordingly, the column was disposed as before, additionally protected by the broken ground in front, and the hills on ei-

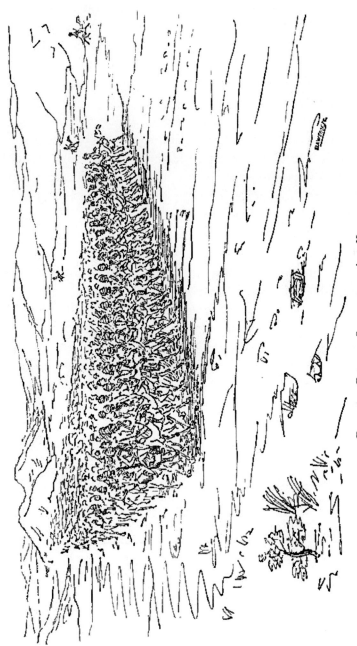

BETWEEN GEBEL ES SERGAIS AND ABU KLEA.

ther flank crowned with sentries. It happened to be my turn for outpost duty; and little did I think, when scrambling my rounds that night in pitch darkness, that some nine or ten thousand of the enemy were within half a day's march of us. Everybody was firmly convinced we should have no fighting till we got to the river, if then; and no one anticipated much of a resistance, least of all in the desert.

Next morning we started before daybreak, and pursued our way over a large gravelly plain, sand-drifts alternating with stretches of level black rock. Expecting to make the wells of Abu Klea by the evening, the column halted about eleven in a small valley at the far end of the plain, just where the ranges of hills (a mile off on either flank up till now), approached one another. The track ahead we saw led up a steepish hill over rocky ground, and then through a regular pass commanded by the hills on each side. According to the map, the wells lay some three miles the other side of this pass in a sandy valley.

Directly the Hussars had finished their meal, they were sent ahead to water their horses, who, poor little beasts, hadn't had a good drink since starting from Gakdul. The rest of the force had finished their dinner in comfort, and were resting peacefully, when the order suddenly came to fall in at once and examine arms and ammunition. Then like a flash the report spread from mouth to mouth that the enemy were in sight on the hills commanding the pass, and were evidently prepared to make a fight of it.

CHAPTER 11
Night of the 16th

The column mounted and fell in at once, much pleased at such an unexpected bit of luck. At last we were actually coming to blows with the enemy that so many had regarded as a phantom. Sir Herbert galloped ahead on to some rising ground, and quickly took in the position. With the help of glasses, all the hills and rocks surrounding the pass were seen to be dotted with white-robed Arabs, jumping about and gesticulating violently. That there were plenty of them down below too was clearly proved by an officer of the 19th (Craven, I think it was), who, on turning a corner, ran straight into a crowd of them, and only saved himself by the speed of his pony. Their numbers altogether seemed to be about 2,000, allowing for half that number to be in reserve behind the rocks. The General saw at once that it would be folly to attempt going straight along the track, as there the enemy had us at their mercy from their position on the hills; he therefore deployed the fighting force into line of columns, baggage-train immediately in rear, and advanced the whole slowly up the broken hills, immediately above the valley where we had been resting.

We shortly came on to an open stretch, and there the brigade was halted, whilst further reconnaissances were being made and the plan of advance settled on. The ground we were on was a brown, rocky slope, cut up into innumerable mounds and small hills, most difficult for manoeuvring on; we therefore soon received the order to move on again, and advanced up the stony slope to a bit of flat ground which gave on to the plain beyond. There we closed to jammed column, and dismounted, tightly knee-lashing our camels.

The view from this spot was extensive. In the distance the broad sandy valley of Abu Klea, covered with the everlasting tussocks of yellow grass and mimosa trees, and on all sides steep, rocky hills opening out towards the front; masses of Arabs congregated on every hill-top, just out of range, their white dresses showing up well against the black ground; on our immediate left in a hollow the track which the enemy fondly hoped we would follow, and which they had commanded by small stone works on the hills near. The signallers were already hard at work with their flags, sending back messages from the scouts of the 19th, when we received the order for a company from each regiment to extend and cover our front. This looked like business, and we waited impatiently for further orders. My company (under the command of C——) happened to be extended on the right front flank, and eagerly we watched the niggers dancing about on the hills, some 2000 yards off. C——, a former musketry instructor, with ideas of his own about the effect of long-range fire, was most anxious to experiment on them by means of section volleys, but he couldn't get leave, and had to fall back on theorising.

On our left we saw a strong detachment of Mounted Infantry and Blue-jackets (with their Gardner) climb a hill the other side of the pass, proceed to build a stone wall enclosure, and mount the Gardner therein. This looked like guarding our flanks for defence, and not for action; and so it proved, for the rest of the force now received orders to pile arms, and build a stone wall *zeriba* as quickly as possible. It was already past four o'clock, and the General had determined not to attack till the next day, so we proceeded to secure ourselves for the night. Sentries were posted, and every one else brought stones and built them up on the lines of a sort of irregular *redan*. The ground was solid, with very few loose stones lying about, and though officers and all worked with a will, before the wall was two feet high the sun had already gone down, and twilight was rapidly coming on. Emboldened by the growing darkness, a crowd of the enemy sneaked up to the top of a hill about 1200 yards off on the right flank, and started a dropping long-range fire at us. A couple of guns were at once brought into action, and blazed shrapnel at them, but apparently with not much effect, for the Arabs stuck to their ground.

Darkness coming on, the guns ceased firing, and attention was turned to manning the *zeriba* in expectation of a night attack. The low stone wall did not extend back to the flanks of the baggage and stores, which were close behind on somewhat lower ground, so a hasty abattis was erected of thorny bushes and wire-entanglement to protect them as much as possible. A pannikin of lime-juice and water was served out to each man, and the work (if one might so call it) was then manned in double rank by the whole force.

Although bullets whistled about our heads wherever a light of any sort was visible, not much harm was done, and men composed themselves to sleep with much *sang-froid*. Soon on all sides arose the noise of tom-toms, now far away in the darkness, and now so close that it seemed as if the whole of the enemy must be mustering for attack within three hundred yards; it was very jumpy listening to them, so I put my trust in the outposts and went fast asleep. Twice during the night, some man afflicted with bad dreams jumped up with a yell and started all his immediate neighbours on to their legs, but they were quieted directly and lay down again. Although the dropping fire went on all night, very few bullets found their billet in the *zeriba*, and I think only two men altogether, a Hussar and a camel-driver, were wounded.

Morning broke at last, and great was the desire to stamp about to get warm again; however, the Arabs on the hill-tops had increased during the night and had discovered the exact range. The bullets flew thicker and thicker, and men who jumped up to stretch their legs were not sorry to lie down again under cover of the little wall. Breakfast was eaten, consisting of bully beef and biscuits out of our haversacks, and a gun was mounted in the salient of the *zeriba*. We waited some time for the enemy to attack, but since they did not seem inclined to do so, the flanking party was called in, and Sir Herbert made his preparations for advance.

The General's person seemed a favourite target for the enemy's marksmen, and brought grief to several. The first to fall was Major Dickson of the Royals (attached to the Intelligence Department), shot through the knee. Colonel Burnaby's horse next received a bullet in the fetlock, and was led limping to the rear; then a bullet grazed the temples of Major Gough (commanding the Mounted Infantry), and knocked him senseless, and another one caught Lieutenant Lyall, R.A., in the back; a large proportion of officers already.

Chapter 12

Action of Abu Klea

Sir Herbert's intentions were, briefly, to fight his way to the wells at any cost, leaving a small garrison to protect the baggage and camels in the *zeriba*; the wells once won, to send back for the baggage, feed and water the column, and push on for Metemmeh at once. The ground over which we should have to advance was far too broken to allow of quick manoeuvring in case of sudden attack. He knew that the only formation to successfully resist vastly greater numbers was a square; so accordingly a square was ordered to be formed.

In the centre of the square were to be some thirty camels for carrying water, ammunition, and wounded men, driven by their respective natives. These dispositions made, Sir Herbert quietly came and sat down amongst us, "waiting to give the niggers another chance," as he said. As they did not take advantage of it, the square was rapidly formed up, and at about 10 o'clock we moved out, keeping to the high ground.

A redoubled fire from the Arabs showed that they saw our movements, and soon the hills were alive with them, running parallel to our square and keeping up a hot fire all the time. Men fell right and left, and the whistling of the bullets overhead was incessant. Skirmishers were accordingly told off to the front and flanks, and they succeeded in greatly reducing the enemy's fire. Just at this time our doctor, Magill, was hit by a bullet in the leg as he was attending a wounded skirmisher outside the square, and he and his patient were brought in with some difficulty. We moved at a slow march all the time, in order to allow of the guns

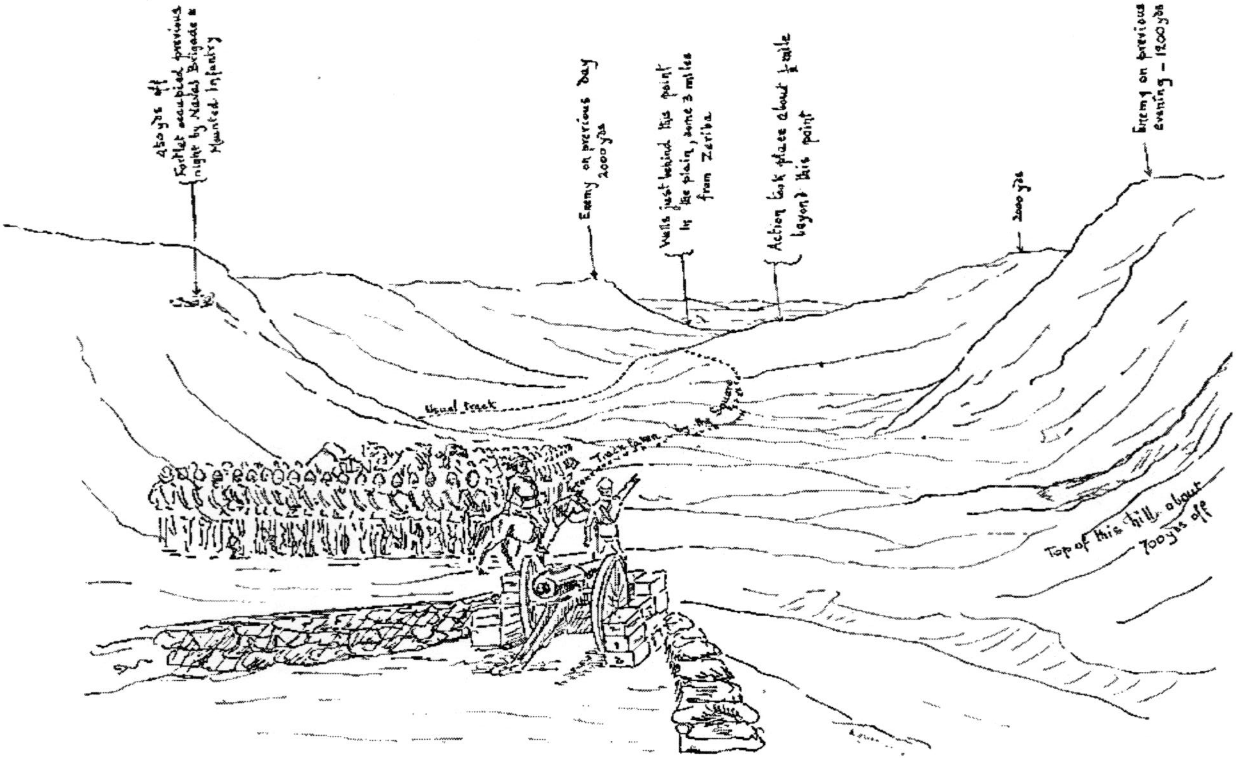
450 yds off
occupied previous
night by Naval Brigade &
Mounted Infantry
Enemy on previous day
2000 yds
Wells just behind this point
in the plain, some 3 miles
from Zeriba
Action took place about ½ mile
beyond this point
2000 yds
Enemy on previous
evening – 1200 yds
Usual track
Track taken by the Square
Top of this hill about
700 yds off

THE SQUARE FORMING UP IN FRONT OF THE ZERIBA.

and camels keeping up. And terrible ground it was for them to get over without disarranging the square: rocky hillocks cut up in places with deep, sandy water-ruts, and very much uphill and downhill, though the leader did his best to keep on level ground. Frequent halts had to be made to enable the doctors to attend to the wounded and mount them in *cacolets*. The camels could not keep up, or together, and were a terrible trouble, sometimes throwing the rear face into great confusion.

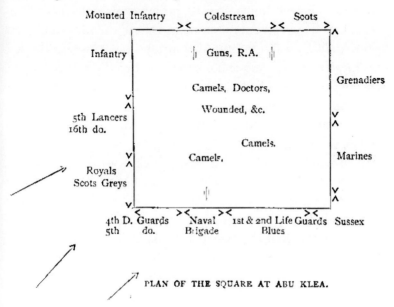

PLAN OF THE SQUARE AT ABU KLEA.

After we had proceeded thus for nearly an hour, the stretchers and *cacolets* getting fuller every minute, a number of green and white flags on long poles were seen some way off in the grass to the left front. Much speculation took place as to what they could be some took them for a burial ground, and others for the position of the enemy's camp. The main body of the enemy was supposed to be on the right, since most of the firing had come from that flank, and the ground there seemed more favourable to attack from.

So much did every one expect the attack from the right, that the officer commanding the Mounted Infantry skirmishers on the left flank (Campbell, of the 60th) sent a message to Sir

Herbert, asking if he might go and take the mysterious flags. The general was on the point of giving leave, when suddenly a hundred more flags uprose in the same place, and the *wady* became alive and black with vast masses of Arabs, who had apparently sprung out of the ground. The square happened to be halted at the foot of a stony knoll when the enemy thus appeared, so it was moved some thirty yards on to a better position on top, and the skirmishers at once called in. With wild yells the Arabs (still about 500 yards off) moved across our left front, in *column of companies*, and disappeared for a moment behind the rocks and grass in the *wady*. In half a minute they reappeared, close on the left rear, *left wheeled into line*, and charged. So quickly was this done, that the skirmishers had barely time to run in before the Arabs were upon them, one unfortunate man of the 60th, an officer's servant who was not in good training, being speared before he reached the square.

In moving the square up this hillock several tired camels, with their loads of wounded, had been left outside, lying down at the foot of the slope; the native drivers could not get them on to their legs, so bolted into the square to save their own skins when the enemy charged. It looked like certain death for the wounded, and no doubt would have proved so if R——— (an officer of the G.C.R.) and one or two other privates of the H.C.R. had not gallantly rushed out and hauled several of the camels in by main force just as the Arabs reached the square. The moment the skirmishers were in, a terrific fire began from the left and rear faces upon the Arabs, volleys rapidly merging into independent firing. I was with my company on the right front, and anxiously my men looked for something beyond a stray skirmishing nigger to shoot at. The camels inside the square obstructed all vision to the fighting flank, and we had already concluded that the fire of the Heavies and Mounted Infantry had swept back the Arabs, when suddenly a terrific shock was felt, accompanied by redoubled yells and firing. I found myself lifted off my legs amongst a surging mass of Heavies and Sussex, who had been carried back against the camels by the impetuous rush of the enemy. Telling the men to stand fast, I forced my way through the jam to see what had happened. Heavies, Sussex, and camels of all sorts were pressing with terrific force on our thin double rank, and it seemed every moment as if it must give; but it didn't.

On getting through to the other side of the press, a gruesome sight was seen. Immediately in front were swarms of Arabs, in desperate hand-to hand fight with our men, hacking, hewing, hamstringing, and yelling like a crowd of black devils on a ground literally piled up with dead and dying. On the right the Mounted Infantry were pouring in their fire with deadly effect, the niggers falling in hundreds. At my side Dr. Briggs, minus his helmet, his patients all killed or scattered, had drawn his sword, and was frantically endeavouring to rally the men near him. I shouted myself hoarse trying to get the men to aim carefully, but my voice was lost in the din. A rain of bullets whizzed dangerously close past my head from the rifles behind into the fighting mass in front. Numbers of the Arabs went down in that hail, and I fear several Englishmen too. Everything depended on the front and right faces standing fast. And well did they stick to it. With the rear rank faced about, the men stubbornly withstood the pressure, and, do what they would, the Arabs could not break in the solid mass of men and camels.

It was too hot to last. At length the enemy, almost annihilated, wavered, turned, and retreated sullenly, our men shooting them down in scores till they disappeared out of range over the hilltops. Many of these brave fanatics turned and charged the square singly, being of course shot down long before they reached it. When we saw the Arabs in full retreat the General gave the word, and we raised cheer after cheer—a little attention evidently not appreciated by the enemy, many of whom turned and shook their fists at us. Oh, that we could have wheeled the front face up on the right of the Mounted Infantry and slated them a bit more! Hardly one of the enemy would have escaped.

This, however, was not to be thought of; for we expected another immediate charge from the right, since certainly not all

ATTACK ON THE LEFT REAR CORNER OF THE SQUARE AT ABU KLEA—THE GARDNER GUN JAMMED.

the enemy we had seen had taken part in the unsuccessful attack. Very soon there was a cry of"Close up! close up! they're coming again!" However, they didn't come, and contented themselves with a dropping long range fire from behind their rocks. Every now and then one of their marksmen would creep down into the broken ground and take pot-shots at the square till he was potted himself. One of our best men (Ormiston, 3rd Grenadiers) was shot by one of these brutes. As he was handing his water-bottle to another man a bullet passed through his friend's hand and pierced his chest. He fell on to me, a torrent of blood gushing out of his mouth. No use trying to staunch it; he was dead in less than a minute.

At length the enemy on the hills melted away, and the fire gradually ceased. Occasionally an Arab, seeing everything was lost, would come out into the open, and expose himself purposely to the bullets of the infidels, and once a horseman charged my company by himself, and got quite close before he was dropped. He was coming straight my way, and I was expecting to get a pot-shot at him, when, to my disgust, a marine bowled him over an awful "crumpler" at an unfairly short range for a rifle.

The square was now moved on to a space clear of dead bodies, and the gaps were closed up. Now that the enemy had disappeared, we had leisure for the sad task of collecting and burying the dead before moving on to the wells. The officers of the G.C.R. collected together for a moment, and we discovered to our mutual joy, that, with the exception of poor Magill, not one of us had been touched. So far so good, but on hearing the death-returns, we were horrified to find that so many of our friends in other regiments had fallen. Nine officers killed and nine wounded, chiefly among the Heavies, with whom we had come out, and whom we knew so well, made a fearful gap amongst our friends. Burnaby, Gough (of the Royals), Wolfe, Carmichael, Law, Atherton, Darley, Piggott, and De Lisle,[1] all killed! St. Vincent not expected to live; and seven or eight others, equally well known to us, wounded!

---

1. These last two sailors.

It was an awful slaughter. On the knoll immediately outside the square lay the bodies of eighty-six Englishmen, wax-like in death and covered with dust and blood. Hardly a square foot but was hidden by the stiffening carcases of men and camels: here B——'s corpse, the head nearly severed from the body; there C——'s, a bullet-hole through the face, and a gaping spear-wound in the neck it was horrible. I did not care to look on any more, lest I should come across the mutilated bodies of more friends. Dead Arabs in hundreds strewed the ground, mostly with a fiendish expression on their still faces. Here and there the Mahdi's uniform and straw cap proclaimed one of superior rank; but the greater part by far were clad in (originally) white garments, wound round the waist, and fastened over the left shoulder the shaven head crowned with a white cotton skull cap. In some cases their clothes had caught fire from the nearness of the discharge of the rifles, and several of the heaps of bodies were smouldering. Arms of all sorts and broken banner-staves were scattered over the field; spears in hundreds, some of enormous length, javelins, knobkerries, hatchets, swords and knives,[2] but no shields of any sort; for the Mahdi, knowing their uselessness against bullets, had ordered them to be left at home, in order to give greater freedom for using the other weapons.

Fatigue parties were now sent out to collect the arms and ammunition strewn about, and to destroy all useless weapons, which was done by breaking up the spears, damaged rifles, etc., and burning them. As many of the dead as possible were buried, and the rest left for a future occasion.

The men were now suffering greatly from thirst, yet there was hardly a drop to give them, nearly all the spare water being used for the wounded. Several men fainted, and many more suffered acutely, their lips turning black, and their tongues swelling so as to cause great pain. It was high time to push on to the wells, so the word was given, and the square moved slowly on very

---

2. I even found a Birmingham bill-hook, with the trade-mark on it, in an Arab's hand, sharp as a razor and covered with blood and hair: how it got there I know not, so I confiscated it for the use of our mess.

slowly, in order to allow the camels and wounded to keep up: 106 wounded was far too large a number to be carried on the few camels we had left who, indeed, were required for medical stores and ammunition; so my company, as being the strongest, was told off to carry them on stretchers. The men were fearfully weak themselves through fatigue and thirst, but stuck to their burdens manfully all the time.

CHAPTER 13

A Terrible Night-March

It was now nearly five o'clock; the men were dead beat, the square was straggling terribly, and the wells were nowhere to be seen. The 19th had been sent ahead on their overworked little horses to look for them, but on this large plain, cut up into *wadies* and covered with scrub, no one knew whereabouts to look. Sir Herbert, in despair, was just going to give the word to retire all that weary way back to the baggage *zeriba*, where a small supply of water was left, when the joyful intelligence came that the Hussars had found the wells, some way off to the left.

The wounded were immediately carried straight off thither, whilst the rest of the force, in perfect discipline, was halted a short way off, to wait till the water could be apportioned out to each corps.

The wells were simply deep holes in the sand, thirty or forty in number, and mostly with one or two feet of water in them. One of my men, a great six-foot-three private, called Rooke, who had taken me under his special protection, soon picked me out in the dusk, and presented me with a huge calabash full of cool milky-tea-coloured water, of the consistency of thin mud. It was delicious! I drank till I was full to the brim, and then felt annoyed that I couldn't hold any more, for the roof of my mouth wasn't soft yet.

When everybody had drunk their fill, a large square was formed for the night on some rising ground close to the wells, for the chances of another attack were not yet by any means over. Three hundred volunteers were then called for from the Heavies, the Mounted Infantry, and ourselves, to march back to the *zeriba* and bring up all the baggage before daylight. They were soon started off, and then began for us quite the coldest night we ever experienced; the wounded must have suffered fearfully. Of course we had no extra clothing or covering of any sort, nothing between us and the freezing night air but a shirt and a very thin serge jacket. I tried to get shelter between two camels, but directly I began to get warm the brutes would feel me and lurch over on top of me, till I was driven into the open again. Hardly a wink of sleep did one of us get that night, and fearfully hungry we were too. Half-a-dozen of us huddled together, giving up sleep as a bad job, and made the time pass by sucking in turns at a solitary pipe—a great preventive of pangs of emptiness in the stomach region. At last the cold grey dawn began to break, and, glad of any movement, we stood to our arms.

No enemy had been seen or heard by our outposts, so the column was formed up and the men allowed to fall out. A herd of lean cattle left by the enemy was soon discovered not far off, and all the native drivers were ordered out in pursuit. The niggers kicked up such a diabolical *hurroosh* in trying to catch them, that they only succeeded in scattering them far and wide, and the Hussars had to ride after them. The cows went such a pace that the ponies could not keep up, and the only way to get fresh beef was to shoot a few and cut them up on the spot. Many dead Arabs were found in the *wadies*, and a good deal of their property too, including a fine pair of those infernal tom-toms, thrown away down a cleft. There was plenty of evidence about in the shape of pottery and old fires, to show that a considerable number of the enemy had been here for some time. Later on, an entire village of tumble-down straw shanties was discovered a little way back, bestrewn with utensils of all sorts, sufficient to prove that thousands of Arabs must have been encamped there for a fortnight, and yet our spies had reported the road quite clear to the river!

At about seven o'clock the baggage was reported in the distance, and, to our happiness, it arrived shortly afterwards; at last we should have something to eat. The camels were quickly knee-lashed and unloaded, and, after gathering as much grass as they could for the poor beasts, the men set to in earnest to prepare their dinners off the few cattle that had been caught. It seems that the baggage *zeriba* had not been attacked at all, the advance of the square having drawn all the Arabs out of the hills after it. Right glad were those left behind to see us again. Their suspense when they heard the tremendous firing going on, out of sight, must have been excessively unpleasant.

The wells, meanwhile, were being taxed to their utmost to supply enough water to fill all our water tanks and skins. Every man had been allowed to fill his water-bottle, and then a guard placed over the wells. Pumps and hose were rigged up, but very soon the supply only came out in the shape of liquid yellow mud. Time was required to allow the water to filter into the holes again, yet time was of the utmost importance to us.

With ravenous joy we welcomed our food after our fast of just two days (the breakfast under fire the day before was hardly to be called a meal), and filled ourselves up with feelings of bliss. If this sort of thing went on, nobody could tell when our next meal would be, so it was best to lay in stores for emergencies. Parade was ordered for four o'clock, which left us just time for digestion and a short snooze. Messengers were then sent off back to Korti with despatches of the battle, and many took this opportunity of sending telegrams off to their friends in England.

All the wounded were to be left behind, with a certain proportion of stores, and a small garrison of Sussex to defend the wells, the rest to make their way at once to the river. Such were the orders; so a stone enclosure was begun, and hospital tents set up for those who were to stay.

By 4.30 we were under way, the General having given out that we should only proceed a short distance and then halt for the night. I was bad luck to it! told off in charge of the regimental stores and baggage, which consisted of seven strings of three camels each, the foremost camel of each string being bestridden by a mongrel nigger. With eight men of the G.C.R. to guard the lot, and plenty of light, it looked easy enough going. I little knew what the night would bring forth.

The track led over a low ridge down on to a huge bare plain, with low scrub and trees just visible in the distance. We expected to reach these, and then halt for the night; but the sun went down, the dusk became darkness, we arrived at the scrub, and yet no orders to halt. Instead of this, the column was shortened and broadened, and perpetual orders were sent back to close up in rear. Not a light of any sort was allowed; orders were passed on in whispers, and strict silence enjoined. It looked very much like a forced march. Past ten o'clock, and no halt! It was evident that Sir Herbert intended to reach the river by the next morning, and we were to march the twenty-six miles intervening during the night.

The perpetual hurrying up of the rear Transport, and lagging of many of the tired-out and famished camels in front, now began to create horrible confusion, and, once scattered, the column got frightfully "mixed;" in the darkness it was useless to try to find one's own men and camels, and Transport, medical stores, regimental baggage, Blue-jackets, niggers, and Commissariat all got hopelessly entangled. My niggers went to sleep, and let their camels drift; the guard got separated and lost in the vast mass of animals and men; I wasn't allowed to shout or bugle them together: altogether my charges were in a nice state. I kept my eye on one of my niggers with a string of water camels, and vowed I wouldn't lose sight of him; somebody got between me and him, and in another moment he had vanished into the blurry outline of the column it was a hopeless business. To make matters worse, we found ourselves at one moment in a dense wood of thorny mimosa trees, which played the blazes with the loads; and I can swear that several times the Pole Star was in front of us, instead of he Southern Cross! We were evidently going in a circle, for occasionally the advance-guard was surprised by finding itself following the rear-guard. The reason was that Sir Herbert had purposely gone off the track, intending to take

a more southerly course, so as to strike the river some way below Metemmeh. Abu Loolah, our friend the robber-chief, and guided the column at first, but the other guides insisted that he was going too far south. Accordingly they were told to go ahead themselves, and succeeded in misleading us and losing our way completely.[1]

It was bitterly cold, and everyone was fearfully sleepy. Men in dozens went to sleep on their camels, and strayed from the column, one or two never being seen again. Thank God, there were no enemy about that night; if the column had been attacked, slaughter must have ensued. Many times was passed up from the rear the word to "Halt in front," whilst the rear-guard picked up stragglers and reloaded broken-down stores; the front of the column then halted by order of the General, whilst the rest closed up on to it, and snatched a few seconds' slumber, till "All right in rear" set the whole in motion once more. Gladly did we hail the first streaks of dawn in the black sky, expecting to find ourselves close to the river by the time the sun was up. It grew lighter and lighter, and eagerly we looked ahead, but no signs of the river yet. My camels drifted together again, more by good luck than good management, and soon we were in our proper places in the reformed column. One of my niggers, a hoary-headed old sinner like a dried-up chimpanzee, was reported to me as having cut his two rear camels adrift in order to go to sleep more comfortably; so he got the *koorbash*, and was condemned to walk all the rest of the way, whilst the others rode.

---

1. So much out of its bearing was the column that it was never discovered what mimosa wood it was we got lost in no one ever came across it afterwards!

CHAPTER 14

Action of Abu Kru

The country we were now on was a vast gravelly slope, covered with scrub and tussocks, evidently reaching in the distance down to the Nile, though we could not yet see it. We hoped to strike it unseen by the enemy some way below Metemmeh, so as to get water and rest awhile before attacking. But our hopes were disappointed. As we advanced, the Hussars brought in word that crowds of Arabs were scattered about the bush, and had already opened fire on them. The column still moved on, but when about four miles off the river (still invisible) such numbers of sharpshooters were seen in the grass round about, that the General determined to rest and feed the men a bit before engaging the enemy. Accordingly, the column was closed up and halted on a bare gravelly space in the scrub, where the ground rose into a low knoll. In the far distance was just to be seen a broad green belt of cultivation, where presumably the river ran, and on the left front a large straggling town, which could only be Metemmeh. Now came the order to unload all the stores and build them up round the knoll. It was very tantalising having thus to halt and make another *zeriba* when so close to the river, and many growls were heard. "Why can't we go right ahead to the Nile? We can do without breakfast for another five or six hours."

However, the British soldier is never happy without his grumble, and very soon the camels were jammed up and tightly knee-lashed, and a wall of biscuit-boxes and saddles built up round them. Bullets kept spattering in on us from invisible marksmen in the long grass all the time, and many was the *Fft, fft!* into the mass of camels. A company was therefore extended along a low ridge fifty yards in front of the *zeriba* to try to keep down the fire, but it was hard work; the only objects to aim at were the puffs of smoke in the scrub, seven or eight hundred yards off, or a dark figure now and then creeping from bush to bush.

It was now nearly nine o'clock, and just about this time happened a terrible disaster. Sir Herbert Stewart, while superintending the arrangements of the *zeriba*, received a bullet in the groin, and dropped mortally wounded. It was a fearful blow to us all, when we heard of it. Leaving out of the question the personal feelings of the whole force, who were, every one of them, devotedly attached to him, it was a catastrophe at a most critical time, since it left the column unexpectedly without a head. Burnaby, next in seniority, had fallen at Abu Klea, and so the command devolved on Sir Charles Wilson, the diplomatic messenger intended by Wolseley to communicate with Gordon at Khartoum. The sad news was kept strictly secret, and only by degrees did it ooze out amongst the officers that poor Sir Herbert had received his death wound, and that his death was only a question of a few hours.

We now received orders to occupy a ridge of ground about sixty yards distant on our right front, and build a tiny work of boxes and saddles there to command the ground beyond it. Volunteers, officers and men, ran out with boxes across the bullet-swept ground, and the fortlet soon rose to a respectable height. Several of the builders were knocked over here, and I personally had a very near squeak of it. I happened to be just at this time with my company on the ridge, covering the building of that work, and was directing the shooting to the best of my abilities. Every one of my men was extended flat on his stomach, potting anything in the shape of niggers or smoke; so as the enemy's bullets were whistling close over our heads, I prudently assumed the same position at first, but found I couldn't bring my field-glasses to bear comfortably. Accordingly I sat up, and was prospecting round satisfactorily, when suddenly I received a violent blow in the pit of the stomach. I staggered up, and immediately fell down flat—my wind was entirely gone, so I lay and gasped. A couple of my men immediately rushed up, caught hold of me, and, at a sepulchral "Take him away," from C——, bore me off between them at a fast "double" for the hospital. My first idea was that I was badly hit, but somehow I didn't seem to feel the bullet inside; the further, too, I went, the better I felt, and by the time we arrived at the *zeriba* I had recovered just sufficient breath to gasp out to the men that I didn't think I was very bad. So I clambered over the wall of saddles and things, and sat down to get my wind and see what damage had been done. It was chiefly to my clothes; the brass button that had saved my life was carried away, ditto watch and compass (that had been connected by a steel chain through the button-hole), and my pockets were half torn away. Further investigation only revealed a large bruise just over my wind. It must have been a ricochet bullet (C—— said he saw it hit the ground in front of me) coming obliquely, but, *racco* or not, it was as near a squeak as I ever wish to have.

When the biscuit-box work was finished, it was garrisoned with about twenty men, and the rest of us retired into the *zeriba*. It was now past eleven, yet no signs of advancing. The enemy had largely increased in numbers, and a continuous rain of bullets went into and over the camel *zeriba*. Every other minute a dead or wounded man was carried past on a stretcher. The men were all fagged out, and although told to help themselves from the boxes in front of them, preferred trying to sleep to eating red stringy beef and dry biscuits, with no water to wash it down. I tried in vain to get a wink of sleep between two camels, but the brutes wouldn't let me, and shifted their positions whenever I got comfortable. Scores of camels were shot; you would hear that sickening *Fft!* go into a camel close by you, and see the poor brute patiently lying there, with a stream of blood trickling from his shoulder or neck. After a time his head would drop lower and lower, till the neck got that peculiar kink in it that betokens the approach of the end, and over he would roll, quite

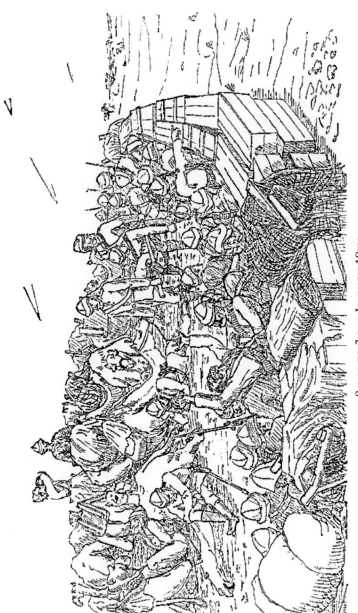

8 A.M. TO 3 P.M. JANUARY 19TH.

silently. They never bellowed or tried to move when they were hit; nothing but an occasional shake or shiver would tell that a bullet was in them. Cameron, the special correspondent of *The Standard*, was killed just about this time; poor St. Leger Herbert was found stiff and cold amongst the camels shortly afterwards another valuable man gone.

At length, about 3.30, Sir Charles made up his mind that it was no use waiting for reinforcements,[1] and that the whole force could not fight its way successfully to the river, encumbered as it would be with wounded and stores; the only alternative was the risky one of half of us fighting our way on foot, whilst the baggage remained behind with the other half. It was neck or nothing, for the fighting force could only muster some 900 bayonets, and the enemy were swarming round in thousands. I must say it looked as risky a business as it well could; we all felt it was exceedingly doubtful if the two halves of the force would ever see each other again, but yet it was the only thing possible to be done. Accordingly a square was formed as shown opposite, and moved out from the camel *zeriba* in a southerly direction, keeping as much as possible in the open, so as to repel any sudden attack from the scrub. Just before starting, our Adjutant (Crutchley) was dropped with a bullet through his right thigh, and his place was filled by Herbert. Leaving behind us part of the Heavies, the 19th, the guns, Blue-jackets, stores, and ammunition, we advanced at the slow march as before, to enable the camels and wounded to keep up. Numbers of men dropped, and amongst the G.C.R. happened many narrow escapes. One of my men (Woods) had armed himself with a spade, since a sprained shoulder prevented him from using his rifle. He held it up before his face, and laughingly remarked to a friend that it would make a capital cover, when bang came a bullet against it and knocked it out of his hand! Another man was knocked down by a bullet lodging in his bandolier. M—— got one through his helmet, D—— one on his scabbard, and N—— a stone, which nearly broke his ankle.

---

1. Lord Wolseley was popularly supposed to be following not far behind, with more troops.

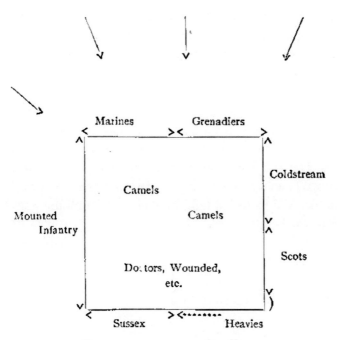

PLAN OF THE SQUARE AT ABU KRU.

I happened to be walking alongside C——, when suddenly he gave a terrific jump, and clapped his hand to his face: a bullet had skimmed through his beard, and passed over his shoulder. Still we moved on, slowly, very slowly, avoiding all dips and hollows which might contain niggers, and every now and then halting to send a few volleys wherever the smoke appeared thickest. At length the Arabs began to collect in large bodies in front, and the long-wished-for moment arrived. "Thank God! they're going to charge!" was the sigh of relief on all sides; and on they came. Several thousand had massed on the slopes on the left front, and they came straight at us. The square was at once halted, and volley after volley poured into the black mass. As they got within 400 yards, the volley-firing became a continuous roar of musketry, and hundreds fell beneath the well directed fire of the Mounted Infantry and ourselves. Aiming low, and firing steadily as on parade, our men mowed the Arabs down like grass; not one got within eighty yards of the square. At last the masses of the enemy in reserve, seeing the fate of the charging lines, wavered, scattered, and bolted over the hills towards Metemmeh, and the river was won!

After a short halt, to allow of a reconnaissance being made as to the best point to strike the Nile, the square moved on again, and soon in the growing dusk a silver streak was visible here and there in amongst the green belt, but still a couple of miles off. The order was now given to push on with all possible speed, to reach it before dark, but yet our pace could not exceed a slow march. The sun went down, and the twilight became almost darkness. Thank goodness, a two-days-old crescent was shining in the sky, and its feeble light guided us through the gravel hills right to the brink of the Nile.

The men were as wild with joy as their exhausted condition would allow. The wounded were held up for one look at the gleaming river, and then hurried to the banks. Still, perfect discipline was observed. Not a man left his place in the ranks

AFTER ABU KRU (PRIVATE ROOKE, OF THE QUEEN'S COMPANY).[2]

2. The bayonet must have been bent by a bullet, as we did not come to close quarters; the man himself could not account for it.

until his company was marched up to take its fill. The front face having drunk itself full was marched to relieve the rear face, and so on, in order that, in case of attack, no flank should be left undefended. However, all was as silent as the grave, and the enemy disturbed us not. In the distance was still heard the faint noise of tom-toms, but most of us were too sleepy to pay any attention to them. A chain of sentries was established on the slopes overlooking the square, and in two minutes the force was fast asleep. So dead tired was every one that I verily believe a horde of yelling niggers would not have awakened us. It was a sleep as is the sleep of a hog; even the cold could not keep us awake.

CHAPTER 15

Back to the Zeriba

Before day broke next morning we stood to our arms in expectation of a possible attack, but whop the sun rose it showed no signs of the enemy. Thoroughly refreshed by our long sleep, and with an unlimited supply of water close by, the first thing to be done was to bring the rest of the force to the enjoyment of like blessings. But before that could be done a strong natural position had to be found wherein to encamp the column when it arrived at the river. Accordingly, part of the Heavies, Mounted Infantry, and ourselves "fell in," and advanced in extended order through several villages on the high ground in the direction of Metemmeh, feeling our way carefully. Not a soul was to be seen; everything had been taken out of the huts food, utensils, forage, everything; the villages were quite deserted.

After some deliberation, we were halted in a village (or rather collection of mud huts) called Gubat, on a slope some four hundred yards from the river, and part of the Heavies told off to entrench themselves there, and hold it at all risks. The programme was then given out that the wounded were all to be fetched up to the village from the position of the night before, and the Heavies were to defend them, whilst the rest of the advanced force returned with water to the camel *zeriba*, and brought up the whole of the stores and troops remaining. There was a question as to whether we ought not to attack Metemmeh at once, and give the Arabs another good hiding before they had recovered from the one of the day before. However, it was deemed too risky; Metemmeh was just about five times the size it was expected to be; we could only have mustered some six hundred men, hadn't had any food for just forty-eight hours, and street-fighting would have entailed many wounded, for whom we had no transport. The idea was therefore wisely given up, and we started for the *zeriba* directly the camel-tanks were brought up filled.

With the water-camels in mass in the centre, flanked by the G.C.R. at the right front and Mounted Infantry at the left rear corner in squares, we pushed on fast over the two miles intervening, keeping a sharp look-out for the enemy. Plenty of them were seen about the field of yesterday's battle, hurrying to and from Metemmeh like a swarm of ants; but as they seemed only to be carrying off the wounded and dead, we did not fire on them. Through our glasses we could see them bearing beds and water about, men, women, and children, all in a great state of excitement, especially when we passed between them and Metemmeh. They seemed quite disorganised, and lid not attempt to attack us, so we continued our larch in peace till we got close up to the *zeriba*. Then many of those left there all night hurried out and welcomed us heartily, and cordial were the greetings indulged in all round. They must have had a bad time of it in the *zeriba*; they told us that when the square went out it looked like going to certain death. Swarms of the enemy that *we* could not see rose out of the scrub and followed us. The guns and Gardner did their level best, and dispersed many of them, but when the square disappeared from sight and violent firing was heard for some moments, and then silence, they said the suspense was awful. The only way they knew that we were safe was that they were not attacked after that, so concluded we had arrived in safety at the river.

"All's well that ends well!" and in a very short time the whole force was hard at work wolfing down a good solid meal of tea and bully. After that orders were given to load up all the camels left with the stores, and return as soon as possible. The work was hard, for all stores, boxes, and saddles were built up round the *zeriba*, and over a hundred of the camels were dead. The contents of many of the boxes were lying scattered about, and the camels were stiff and tired with fatigue and hunger; added to this, many of the saddles were broken, so several hours elapsed before everything was ready to start. I looked eagerly for my own camel, Potiphar, and found him calmly gazing about him in the same spot where I left him, not damaged in the least, and as bad-tempered as ever. Only my sheepskin and blankets had disappeared, but since they had probably gone for the wounded I did not mind: several of the others had had their *zuleetahs* rifled, probably by the native drivers on the look-out for loot; so I was in comparative luck.

Our first inquiry had of course been after Sir Herbert, and to our delight we were told he was still alive, and doing well. It was a pleasant surprise, for the doctors had said he could not possibly live through the night. The bullet had entered his groin, and, passing round, had lodged under his spine in a, so to speak, safe place; as long as no inflammation or fever set in, he was safe. The rest of the wounded were doing fairly well, and were fit to be carried to the river. I went to see poor Crutchley, who was in such good spirits that I had no idea his wound was so bad as it really was.

The column started as soon as it was ready, all on foot in case of attack. After repeated halts for closing up, we came in sight of the Nile again, and the 19th Hussars dashed ahead to give their poor little horses a drink. The whole of them had been fifty-eight hours, and many seventy-two hours, without a drop of water! The next to be watered were the camels, who had all been very nearly seven days without a drop. It was quite a pleasure seeing the poor brutes make for the river and stand there sucking it up without moving. Potiphar remained fourteen minutes with his nose in the water, and then began eating the green cotton plant all round us as if he would never stop. One of my baggagers was so much affected by the sight of the river, that he took a mouthful and dropped stone dead.

It had now got pitch dark, but numbers of fires had been lighted in the village by the time the camels were all watered, so

I tethered all my baggagers round a big heap of straw and green stuff, and made my way to the mess. The houses in the village were really quite decent, far superior to the dirty mud hovels which constitute a village in Lower Egypt. They were built of a sort of concrete and surmounted by conical or horizontal roofs of straw and *dhurra* stalk, the walls averaging about eleven feet high. The better huts were divided into two or more rooms, very clean and neat perhaps owing to every portable article having been taken away before we arrived.

Orders had been issued for a parade at 4.30 next morning to see about taking Metemmeh; so obviously the only thing to do was to have a good feed all round and get as much sleep as possible in the interval. Our indefatigable little old cook, Carlo,[1] had prepared a capital meal by the time we were ready for it, and in a very short time after its consumption most of us were fast asleep. Occasionally a house, or rather its roof, would catch fire, and alarm us a bit, and then there was a little excitement till it was put out, but that was all; the enemy left us in peace. The night was horribly cold, and I felt the loss of my blankets keenly. The only thing I could get hold of was a straw mat, and that wasn't warm: luckily Jacky came sniffing about, so I got him to lie alongside me, and we kept each other warm till the morning.

---

1. A Maltee who had served in the Crimea.

Chapter 16

Gordon's Troops Arrive

At 4.30 a.m. the force paraded, nominally for the purpose of taking Metemmeh, but, as it turned out, the manoeuvres were limited to a reconnaissance in force. The ground we paraded on was just outside Gubat, about a mile and a half south-west of Metemmeh, with two straggling villages between us and the town. The troops consisted of the Heavies, now reduced to about two hundred and forty, the Mounted Infantry, and ourselves, together with two guns, a few Engineers, and a proportion of ammunition and hospital camels; total, about seven hundred and fifty of all ranks.

The Guards' Camel Regiment and Mounted Infantry extended each a couple of companies, and, with the Heavies in reserve, we advanced slowly over the broken ground through the villages, examining carefully every hut: not a soul was visible there, all the inhabitants having decamped the previous day into Metemmeh, taking with them their goods and chattels. As we passed through the second village and got in view of Metemmeh, crowds of Arabs were seen running about just outside the town. "Here's a grand chance," thought C——, the former *musketoon*, who was in command of the extended company of Grenadiers, and he forthwith called out twenty of our best marksmen. "Fire five volleys, at 2,000 yards ready," and down they rent, taking careful aim at the masses of niggers, The effect of the volleys was extraordinary. At that enormous distance we saw, with the help of our glasses, some two or three Arabs drop, and all the rest skedaddle as fast as their legs would carry them into the town, dropping their household goods as they went. The moral effect must have been great, for in two minutes, with the help of a few shells from the guns, they had all disappeared within the walls.

If we had had sufficient troops, our proper course would have been to get round the town and rush it from the undefended side on the east; but we could not afford to run the risk of being cut off from Gubat and our stores, so had to content ourselves with getting within a thousand yards and peppering it with our little guns. For a short time a company of Mounted Infantry and a few Sappers were told off with the guns to take up a position between two huts on a knoll from whence to shell the enemy out of his defences, but the little seven-pounders made no visible impression. Accordingly they were withdrawn, and the whole formed up in square and moved in a southerly direction round the town, in order to find a practicable place for assault. As far as could be seen, the enemy had loopholed all the walls, and had even constructed a round fortlet on our side, from whence they kept up a spattering fire. A company was therefore extended in front of the square, as skirmishers, but could not do much in the way of keeping the fire down, as none of the enemy were visible. Our shells, too, did very little damage, for they went through the walls like paper, not meeting sufficient resistance to cause them to explode; when they did burst, they only knocked a hole in the cement walls, without setting the place on fire—there was nothing combustible bar the roofs, and, even when one did catch fire, for all practical purposes a hut without a roof was nearly as good as a hut with one. Thus half in hour was spent in slowly moving round the town, during which time nothing serious on either side was effected. As we got round between the town and the river, there was suddenly a heavy report from the walls, and a round stone shot, as we afterwards discovered it to be, whizzed over our heads and buried itself in the ground close by. This was entirely unexpected, and most unfair, we thought it at the time. However, not much time was given us to think; for a second and third followed the first, each nearer than the one before. The third smashed a camel's jaw, and fell into the square, and the fourth wounded a man and killed a camel. It was time to move, so the square was rapidly deployed, and, wheeling into open column, we marched back just out of range of that infernal Krupp gun.

At that moment there was a joyful shout of "Gordon's steamers;" and in truth we saw the Egyptian flag at four mast-heads, just above the *dhurra* stalks towards the river. Not a moment was lost by our gallant allies; they ran their guns on shore, and hastened towards us, about 200 of them. They were all fine men, mostly coal-black negroes, attired in a fez, a shirt, a cartridge-belt, and a rifle. Nothing could have exceeded their readiness to fight, and they were disgusted on learning we did not intend to take the town yet. It was marvellous to see what good soldiers Gordon's genius had made out of this rough material; their little brass guns were hard at work alongside ours in less than three minutes from their appearance, whilst their Infantry spread out and kept up a hot fire on the town, not in the least minding the continual whiz of the bullets all round them.

We all felt much cheered by the steamers arriving—it seemed next thing to meeting Gordon himself, whilst finding these keen allies after our late hard work was morally a great relief; besides this, they formed a valuable addition to our small force. The news the steamers brought was that Gordon was still holding out, though woefully short of provisions and men; that the Mahdi was pressing him close, and also that 3,000 of the enemy were not two days' march off Gubat, determined to avenge Abu Klea. Under the circumstances, Sir Charles Wilson, after a short council, determined not to assault the town, but to take up a strong position at Gubat, and hold it at all hazards against the approaching force. The guns were therefore allowed to pepper away for an hour or so, to try to effect some damage somewhere, whilst the Infantry remained under cover of some rising ground in rear of the guns. A company of the G.C.R. was ordered to support the guns at the two huts aforesaid to reply to the enemy's fire, which had been concentrated on them. And just there Major Poe of the Marines was hit by a bullet which smashed his thigh. He would persist in wearing a red coat, saying his grey one was not fit to be seen, and this naturally attracted the Arab marksmen. At length we got the command to retire, and did so slowly, by alternate battalions, setting fire to the houses on the way. We were back at Gubat by noon, feeling that we had spent an unsatisfactory morning.

USEFUL ALLIES.

After the men's dinner we all paraded to strengthen the position. Various counsels prevailed for a time; but at last it was settled to build a fort at the river, to hold the whole force except the Guards' Camel Regiment, which was to establish itself in the village of Gubat, on the top of the slope, so as to prevent the enemy from taking possession of it and "slating" the lower fort. Accordingly all camel-saddles were taken to the banks, and a rough defence was made with them, enclosing the stores and hospital. A small fort was also begun by our men in the village, by pulling down some of the huts and building walls with the debris—but not much progress could be made before nightfall. Luckily the night passed without any signs of the enemy, and the next day was devoted to the continuance of the work. Sir C. Wilson had sent out one of the steamers on the previous afternoon, in order to find out whether the reported enemy were anywhere near; but though she patrolled up and down the river

111

that evening, and the whole of the next day, she failed to find them, so returned to Gubat directly she had made sure that the force was not likely to be immediately molested.

Meanwhile preparations were going on for Sir Charles's journey to Khartoum. Coal for the steamers of course there was none, and the only wood to be got was by destroying the sakiyehs[1] all along the banks and cutting them up. This was most troublesome, for it entailed cutting-parties, armed covering-parties, and loss of much valuable time, besides which the wood was hard and bulky, and burned very quickly. Stores and arms were put on board for the plucky defenders of Khartoum, and by nightfall all was ready for an early start.

Next morning Sir Charles started at daybreak in two steamers, taking with him twenty of the Sussex, and about 150 of Gordon's blacks. In his messages Gordon had repeatedly said that the presence of a few red-coats at Khartoum would work wonders; so the twenty men were selected from the Sussex, as having been longest up country, and rigged out in red jumpers belonging to our men, as they had none of their own. They were not, as might be expected, a particularly good fit.

---

1. Water-wheels.

CHAPTER 17

Outpost Duty

The orders given to Sir Herbert by Lord Wolseley being that he was to establish himself strongly on the river, and send back a convoy for more stores, so as to make his station a concentrating depot for the final advance on Khartoum, it was determined to follow them out as far as possible, though the original orders, of course, had not taken into account the enormous losses in men and camels we had suffered. Accordingly a convoy was started off back to Gakdul on the evening of the 23rd, composed of all the camels fit to go, escorted by 300 mounted Coldstream, Marines, Heavies, and Mounted Infantry. It was hard work getting the camels together, for during the two previous days, whilst we were building our forts and wandering around Metemmeh, hundreds of the poor famished beasts had strayed in search of the forage and water they stood so much in need of. Scores had died, and their bodies, lying about rotting in the sun, did not add to the beauty of the scene. Those picked out as fit to go were in an appalling state of thinness and sore backs, but there was no help for it. None of the saddles had enough padding for their diminished humps, yet they were crammed on as best they might, and added much to the sores already there. About 400 camels were enrolled in the baggage-train, and these, with the 300 of the escort, left the force behind with barely 100 (in an awful state of decay) for all purposes.

With the convoy and Sir C. Wilson's party gone, the grand total was reduced to about 54 officers and 870 men, including medical staff, commissariat, natives of all sorts, and the remainder of Gordon's Soudanese, besides about 120 wounded. As may be easily imagined, this did not give us many spare rifles, so there was all the more reason for entrenching ourselves securely. Down at the river the lines of a strong parapet were laid down round the hospital and stores, and every one was set to work on it. In our position at the top of the slope, the fort we had started was found too large for our now reduced numbers to hold, so three huts were selected in a convenient position, and walls were strongly built up of rubble and debris between them. The men of course grumbled at having to pull all their work down again; but Tommy Atkins always works the better for a good growl, and very soon the walls began to rise in our new fort, officers and men all taking their share at amateur masonry. It was hard work, certainly, building six hours a day against time in the broiling sun, but I am certain we were all the better for it. Our fort being on a gravelly hill we got every puff of cool wind going, and no dust to speak of. We were well off, too, for water, having a good cool well not fifty yards from the fort. Down by the river-side they fared worse; the ground they were on was very damp at night, whilst during the day they were overwhelmed with clouds of dust. The consequence was that the men on the banks got seedy, and many went into hospital, whilst all ours kept strong and fit, hardly one falling sick.

When off duty we generally strolled "down-town" to the river fort to hear the latest "shaves," and to visit the hospital. Most marvellous air it was for cures: spear-wounds and bullet-holes closed up wonderfully quickly, and men that had been given up entirely recovered, and hobbled about in an extraordinarily short time. There were some curious cases. One man in the Heavies had received a bullet in the back of his neck, and it was cut out under his tongue! Another man in my company, Coyne, was saved by his knife, which turned off into his flanks a bullet which must have otherwise broken his thigh. Both these men had already begun to struggle about, and were on the high-road to recovery. There were numbers of similar cases with which the doctors were much pleased: they attributed the rapid cures to the dry air.

THE INTERPRETER OF THE MOUNTED INFANTRY.

It would have been very interesting to have kept a diary of shaves. The most marvellous stones were started, and they found ready credence: that Wolseley was only two days off; that the Mahdi was dead; that 15,000 of the enemy were advancing from Berber, and would be here in three days; that 6,000 more were coming from Khartoum; that we were to attack and take Metemmeh at once; that the Mahdi's troops had all bolted; that the Berberines had all come over to our side—everything but the truth. Some of us used to start shaves on purpose to see them come back with variations.

During the daytime a chain of vedettes of the 9th Hussars was kept up round the position, and perpetual "potting" went on. Stray Arabs would sconce themselves all day at a safe distance, and try to pick off the vedettes, who replied at intervals with their carbines. None of our men were ever hit, and only once did a Hussar report, with much glee, that he had shot an

Arab at 1,000 yards: unfortunately no one believed him, so it did not count as an authentic kill. At sunset the Cavalry came in, and we relieved them on outpost duty on the slopes round our fort. At first it was rather hard work, for we had to find (out of the G.C.R. alone) two subalterns and seventy men every night; this, out of four subalterns and 223 men, meant for us only every other night in bed, which was somewhat fatiguing, to say the least of it. Luckily this system did not last long, and it was soon changed to one officer and twenty-four men. The reason why at first we had to have so many men out was that the chain of sentries extended round the whole position, river fort and all; now orders were given for each fort to find its own sentries, a much simpler plan. Our picquet was therefore divided into eight posts of three men each, of which one man at a time was on sentry go, and when the officer or sergeant went his rounds (every hour), he took a man from each post up to the next, and sent him back, and so round the chain. These relieved themselves every two hours, thus obviating the necessity of N.C.O s and reliefs marching out to them, and reducing the number of patrols necessary. Their orders were, in case of attack, not to try to resist the enemy, but to give the alarm and bolt back into the fort. The enemy, however, never appeared; we heard afterwards they expected us to attack them nightly, like we expected them, and so confined their demonstrations to beating tom-toms all night outside their town.

Those tom-toms got on one's nerves, especially when on outpost duty at night. You would hear them growing louder and louder in the darkness till they seemed to come quite near till you expected a momentary attack, and then they would die away again in the distance, only to advance again ten minutes afterwards with their infernal *tap! tap! tap! tap! tap! tap!* how we used to curse them! I don't think they were highly approved of in Metemmeh either, for one morning a young black lady came in from the town, declaring she really couldn't stay there any longer, for the row that the dervishes made every night parading the streets with their tom-toms kept all decent people awake!

Natives used sometimes to walk in from the parts near, offering cattle or corn for sale, or saying they wished to be protected from the Mahdi, but doubtless many of them were spies, for they disappeared mysteriously after a few days. They brought news too, sometimes true, generally false, about Khartoum and the intentions of the Emir of Metemmeh; but of course it was never safe to trust them. We wondered often who was really in command at Metemmeh: the natives always said this man, the Emir Nusri, but he must have had a European adviser to have defended the town with earthworks and small forts as he did. At Abu Klea three separate signallers swore to having seen a European in a white helmet and jacket and jack-boots, directing the attack of the enemy, and this pointed again to his existence. One mysterious occurrence happened. I happened to be on outpost duty one very dark night, when, on going my rounds, a sentry reported that a man had just come from the direction of our fort, behind him, and had passed through the line of sentries towards Metemmeh. Of course he challenged, but received no answer; the third time he challenged he threatened to fire, when the figure answered "Friend," in (so the sentry said) a foreign accent, and disappeared over the hills towards the town. My patrol and I gave chase in the direction indicated, but as we could not see three yards in front of us it is not surprising that we did not capture the gentleman in question.

Meanwhile our stores were getting small by degrees and beautifully less. We had started from Gakdul with three weeks' provisions; but the terrible waste entailed at the Abu Kru *zeriba* added to our loss in camels had already caused the daily rations to be reduced. Anything extra in the shape of food was most acceptable. I remember one night a fat sheep innocently straying into my arms, as I was going my rounds; we lived on him for three days, and very good he was. Even with such strokes of luck, however, the stores would only last till the 2nd February; after that we should have to eat our camels it was therefore doubly necessary to keep them in health for eating diseased camel did not sound appetising.

The poor brutes had now water enough and to spare, but hardly anything to eat they had long ago devoured all vegetation within reach, and every day it became a harder task to supply them. Accordingly a strong forage-party was sent out daily with about forty camels, to bring back loads of green-stuff from wherever they could get it. This occasionally led to skirmishes, and battles on a small scale. Parties of the enemy used to hide in the *dhurra*, the other side of the river, and keep up a dropping fire; sometimes they even ventured to skirmish around on our bank, but never came to close quarters. No one on our side was ever hit, so we came to look on these little encounters as an agreeable diversion in the morning's work. On these expeditions we used to loot everything we came across, but as all the villages near were perfectly empty, the spoils were generally confined to picking beans and lentils for the mess, and seizing as many *angarebs* (native wooden bedsteads) as we could carry off. The villages were far better than many I have seen in Egypt, and, for the matter of that, better than a good many at home— very clean, strongly built, plenty of room between the huts, and well laid out, with extra big huts for the chief man, the school, and the assembly-room really highly civilised. The amount of green-stuff brought back one would have thought ample for the camels; but they wolfed it up and asked for more. That they needed it badly was plainly shown by the state of their bodies; in several cases they were in such a terrible state that their ribs *literally* came through their skin, and became brightly polished by the friction of the baggage-saddles.

Up in our fort we were fairly comfortable the three huts at the angles were allotted as mess hut, guard-room, and store-room respectively. The former proprietor of the mess hut had kindly left his double *angareb* in it, and this served us for a table; in the tiny enclosure outside all the officers lived, each provided with his *angareb*, and at night all the men slept in the remaining portion of the fort. There was so little room over, that it was a blessing having twenty-five men on outpost every night, and when a gun and its attendant gunners were sent up, it was a very tight fit indeed. In one sense it was useful being crowded like this, for it kept us warm at night, the weather being horribly cold, especially just before dawn. I know I wore an extra waist-coat, a greatcoat, and two blankets at night, and even then had to wrap my waterproof sheet round me to keep warm; whilst during the daytime it got so hot, that working from twelve to three was out of the question unless there happened to be a cool breeze blowing.

Our little fort was thus amply manned in case of emergency; but, as it happened, we were never attacked. The only notifica-tions at night we had of the enemy's existence were those ever-lasting tom-toms. Once, on the evening of the 28th, we heard rapid intermittent firing of guns and rifles in Metemmeh, but put it down to some religious festival; we were doomed to be badly undeceived in a very short time.

On the 31st of January, the convoy arrived from Gakdul, with stores, three guns, and a couple of mails, but, alas! no instructions whatever from headquarters, and no fresh camels. Neither did they bring any news: they had not heard of or seen any of the enemy; the wounded at Abu Klea were doing well, and had not been attacked; St. Vincent and Guthrie had died of their wounds; but that was all. Duller, whom we so eagerly expected to take command, had not turned up, and our only reinforcements were some more Naval Brigade and the three guns aforesaid. We were somewhat disappointed at these small results of the convoy's journey; but still there was the fresh supply of food, and so far we were all safe; so really there was not much to grumble at. We little knew what news the morrow would bring forth.

CHAPTER 18

On the March Again

Next day, the 1st of February, was a Sunday, and we all paraded as usual for church in our Sunday-go-to-meeting red jumpers and trousers. It struck me at the time that all the staff wore a very serious look, but none of us were prepared for the awful news that they had to impart. Gradually it trickled out amongst the officers that the worst possible catastrophe had happened. *Khartoum had fallen!* and Gordon was probably killed!

Our first feeling was that, if the news were true, the object of the expedition was gone; that all our fighting and the lives of so many of our men had been thrown away for nothing; and that, as usual, the Government had sent us out too late! Our second, that we were in (so to speak) rather a hole; that the besieging hordes of the Mahdi were now let loose, and were not improbably within measurable distance of us, thirsting for an opportunity for avenging Abu Klea. Wolseley, we knew, had not enough spare troops to reinforce us sufficiently to make headway against the thousands of the enemy, and even if he had, couldn't bring them up in time; the river column was not expected for at least another month, and our provisions would certainly not last more than a fortnight or so; altogether it was not a happy prospect. In answer to our eager inquiries as to particulars, we learnt that when Sir Charles Wilson and his steamers had come within sight of Khartoum, they had found it already in possession of the enemy, and, on approaching, had met with such a tremendous fire from the banks and the town itself that it was foolhardy to go any further. They therefore returned at once, and on going down the Shabluka cataract both steamers had been wrecked; the troops were landed and entrenched themselves, whilst Stuart Wortley was sent down in a *nugger* to bring us the news and get assistance. Such, in outline, was what we heard. Nothing definite was known of the fate of Gordon.

What was to be done? It was no use waiting for instructions from Korti, for they might be weeks coming, and meanwhile we should probably be attacked. Obviously the only thing was to fortify our position still more strongly and wait the course of events. The only question was whether we should still further weaken our small force by sending back a convoy and escort for more stores. As, however, it was not for us personally to determine that knotty point, we dropped it, and discussed the main question in all its bearings. What a slap in the face this would be for the Government! Was Gordon alive or dead? If alive, he must be got hold of somehow. Government *must* be kicked out for this! Wonder how many niggers will go for us at once, and when? How this will raise the natives' spirits all over the country! Hope Wolseley has got his plans cut and dried, even for this emergency! How disgusting to be just too late! And many more futile questions and remarks. We had to talk in whispers, for the men were not to be told on any account yet, though it would not be long before they must learn the news.

Orders speedily came for all hands to set to work and strengthen our position still further, and the hard work soon took our minds off brooding on the subject. Gravel buttresses were thrown up against the walls of the fort outside to stop any shells that might otherwise have knocked down the rubble masonry, and a hedge of thorn-bushes was started as an outer circle of defence.

By noon it had been settled to send a convoy back to Gakdul to bring up more stores, and orders were issued to start at moonrise, about eight o'clock. It was to be of much the same proportions as the first three hundred Heavies, Guards, and Mounted Infantry as escort to all the remaining camels fit for carrying a load. Besides the camels for stores, all the sick and wounded possible to be moved were to be sent back, to the number of about one hundred and ten. Our particular contingent consisted of one hundred men, Grenadiers and Scots Guards, including three officers besides myself. Our camels were to be mostly the same that had come in only the day before with the first convoy; they were consequently a very sorry lot. The few that had remained at Gubat looked hardly fit to walk a mile, much less to Gakdul and back, but there was no help for them; the best were picked out and saddled, and by eight o'clock we were all ready to start.

I must say things looked rather bad for those who were to remain; but still, if they were attacked, we knew they could hold out as long as there were walls to cover them. The chief thing to fear was heavy artillery; and we heard the enemy were bringing up big guns from Khartoum. It seemed quite on the cards that we might find the Gubat garrison in small pieces when we came back. But it was no good being dismal about it yet; time enough for that when it happened.

The convoy got off by 9 p.m., and in a very short time we had got out of sight of Metemmeh and any stray Arabs that might be prowling about to intercept us. My post was in command of the rear-guard, and this entailed a good deal of irritating work. Every five minutes you would see a dark mass lying on the ground, whilst the column rapidly disappeared amongst the bushes and hillocks. The rear-guard's particular duty was to set this mass on its legs again, and flog it up, not allowing any stragglers whatever behind. Often several camels were lying about at the same time, minus their burdens, and sometimes minus their drivers. When one had been set on its legs and flogged along, another would break down, and by the time he was in marching order again, the first's load would come off, and necessitate another three minutes' halt before he could proceed. Meanwhile the column was out of sight, and was only to be halted by sound of the bugle till we came up with it. It was an aggravating duty in the extreme. We were very lucky in having a moon at all to guide us; but still it was hard to see any distance through the bushes. Trees, stones, camels, grass, and men were all the same light-grey colour in the moonlight, with intensely black shadows, and the column moving over the soft ground made no noise whatever. As night went on, it got, as usual, bitterly cold. By three o'clock twenty-three dying camels had been left behind; all the spare ones had long ago been used up, and yet the brutes kept on dropping. Till now the saddles and loads of the derelicts had been packed on other camels; but now there were none left strong enough to carry double loads, so saddles and all were left on the sand. We welcomed with joy the first streak of dawn, for the light would allow of the column getting further ahead of the rear-guard, and not necessitate those frequent and irritating halts. An hour after dawn we halted for breakfast in the wide tussocky plain, and devoured our short rations with much relish. The bully had cooled to delicious corned beef during the night, and our only complaint was that there was not enough.

After an hour's halt the convoy was put in motion again, and by midday we had surmounted the ridge and arrived at the camp of Abu Klea. The place was a good deal altered since we had last seen it; several hospital-tents were up, a small fort had been built, surrounded by a dangerously close[1] *zeriba* of thorn-bushes, and the wells had been slightly improved. The small garrison of Sussex, who had already been apprised of the news by special messenger through to Korti, was very glad to see us, but had no news of the enemy at all, or from the rear. Orders were issued at once to clear out all the sick and wounded possible, and, whilst the detachment of Guards was left behind to follow on with the wounded, the M.I. and part of the Heavies went on with the empty transport camels to hurry up the stores from Gakdul, leaving a few Heavies to strengthen the garrison.

The wounded convoy was not long in following them, and before night fell we had passed the battlefield and got clear of

1. On account of its liability to be fired by the enemy in case of attack.

the pass beyond. Scores of dead bodies were still lying about the country, all in a mummified condition, and smelling horribly. The air was so dry that they would not decay properly, but simply dried up in the hot sun and stank. On the actual scene of the fight, to the left of the track, there were still piles of bodies, though hundreds had been taken away and buried. Those in the camp at the wells had told us that, for days after the fight, troops of Arabs used to come down to the field after dark, and bring water and food for their wounded friends who were too badly hit to move. Now, however, here was not a sign of anything living.

My company was now on advanced-guard instead of that awful rear-guard, a much better position in every way. As we got to the top of the pass we could see the transport convoy about three miles ahead in the vast plain; so we pushed on in all haste to reach them before it got dark, and encamp together. Twilight fell, and it was all I could do as advanced-guard to make out the faint camel track; but my doubts did not last long. The leading convoy had now halted, and began to light grass fires, which gave us plenty of beacons in the darkness. As we neared them, the ground got very broken, so I whacked up Potiphar to find a better route for the wounded, who would get horribly shaken and jolted that way. I soon found a sort of level track, and then made a bee-line for the nearest fire to find out particulars of the encampment. The consequence was that I got into terrible grief. Potiphar collapsed into a hole, and sat there roaring; when I had hauled him out by main force and flogged him on, he fell into another and refused to budge, so I left him there and made my way on foot. Eventually I reached the transport, and in a short time our convoy was brought alongside and bivouacked for the night; tea was made and drunk, and soon all were wrapped in a well-deserved slumber.

Next morning reveille did not sound till 6.15 for the wounded convoy, so we arose, much refreshed, in broad daylight a thing we had not done for three weeks. The transport convoy had already started, but our orders were to "take it easy" for the benefit of the wounded, so we grazed our camels and did not move off till nearly eight. The day's march was an easy one, till five o'clock, when we halted about halfway between Gebel es Sergain and Gebel en Nus. Next day saw us again on the track, which we followed to within nine miles of Gakdul, and halted on a fair grazing-ground for our poor steeds, who had had no food except this dry grass since leaving Gubat. The following morning we started again at eight, and got into Gakdul before noon.

CHAPTER 19

Kababish

Right glad were we to see the place again, and more especially to hear that at last we should have definite orders of some sort; for General Duller was there, and was coming back with us to Gubat to take over command of the whole advanced force. The 18th Royal Irish had arrived (on foot) from Korti, and they were also going on with us, but yet no orders had been received from headquarters to direct the movements of the Gubat force. Evidently everything was to be left to Buller's discretion however, we couldn't have had a better man. General Wood was in command at Gakdul of the lines of communication; it was quite a pleasant novelty seeing two real live Major-Generals again, and we made certain that we should now push on with the reinforcements, and take Metemmeh at least, if not advance still further.

The whole of the 6th was spent in grazing and resting our camels, who were all of course fearfully knocked up by their foodless journeys. We had hoped to find a large supply of fresh camels to take us back; but no, the wretched false economy of the Government had borne fruit, and no camels were forthcoming. During the day a convoy of stores came in from Korti, escorted and driven by the Kababish, a friendly tribe who had been hired with their camels to convey stores across to Gakdul. It literally made my mouth water to see these magnificent, well-fed brutes swinging along, each with their small load *balanced* (not tied) on their humps, and driven along in troops by their masters. Real children of the desert these natives looked, with their bright copper skins, handsome features, and thick mops of long black hair. Some of the faces were really quite beautiful, reminding me of a *beau-ideal* John the Baptist: aquiline nose, large, dark eyes, and wild though somewhat mournful expression; as for their figures and muscular development, they were simply perfect. I could have watched them for hours, but had to attend to the more prosaic duties of drawing rations and water for the morrow.

A CHILD OF THE DESERT.

We soon got our orders, which were for ourselves (G.C.R. detachment) and the convoy of stores to start next morning about nine. The 18th were to proceed on foot that night, directly the moon rose, at about 1 a.m., and we should catch them up by the evening. Duller would wait a little longer for despatches from Korti, and join us at Abu Klea, where we were all to concentrate before going on to Gubat.

Accordingly, next morning we got off pretty punctually, and marched on till evening without finding any trace of the Irish except a drummer and a couple of men, who had got lost, and didn't know where their battalion was, or in fact anything about themselves or the country. Immediately afterwards we espied a small party in the distance trotting rapidly towards us; on coming up they proved to be Sir Charles Wilson, Stuart Wortley, and V—— D——, with some Coldstream as escort. They could not stop long, but we gathered from them that Beresford had gone up in his steamer to rescue Sir Charles and his party off their island, and after a very plucky fight (during which he had got a round-shot through his boiler) had succeeded in taking them off. They also brought certain news of Gordon's death, he having been murdered coming out of his room on the 26th. And the steamers arrived at Khartoum on the 28th! It was too disgusting! Sir Charles was making his way to Korti, and had already done a good record sixty-four miles in twenty-seven hours, on decaying camels. No signs of the Irish, so at five we halted for the night.

Next day we caught up the Irish in the sand drifts near Gebel en Nus; they were being led by Cochrane (now Dundonald) of the 2nd Life Guards, who always made a bee-line per compass for his point, without reference to landmarks or tracks: this accounted for Sir C. Wilson's party missing them. After a comfortable night's rest we started for the pass of Abu Klea, just visible in the dim distance, and reached the battle-field about 2 p.m. During the last four days the Heavies left there had raised a big cairn of stones over the graves of our men; but hundreds of the dead enemy were still unburied. It struck me that there seemed more dead lying about then than on the actual day of the fight perhaps because I had a better view from the top of my camel than from the ground on the former occasion; the enemy's loss had been estimated at about 1,300, yet, though scores had been buried, there seemed quite that number still on the ground. On examining the position closely, it was evident that the Arabs had made grand preparations for destroying the column in the pass; shelter-trenches and rifle-pits in abundance, and with many empty cartridge-cases in them, flanked the defile from the rising ground on all sides; there was even a rough attempt at a field-work in one place. It must have rather annoyed them finding their elaborate dispositions of no use, through Sir Herbert taking them in flank and entirely ignoring their plans for his destruction. We searched in vain for interesting relics of the field—but all worth having had been taken long ago, and nothing was left on the bodies but the usual dress of white (?) sheet, and skull-cap.

On reaching the hospital camp, we found nothing further of interest had happened. Everyone was very anxious to know whether Duller intended to hold Gubat or retreat at once, but as he had not confided his plans to us, we could not enlighten the company. By the time we had fed the men and posted the usual entries it was bed-time (7.30 p.m.), so we turned in. Next morning Duller arrived with the 18th, a small convoy of stores, and the escort of M.I. He had just received his despatches, these being the first ones sent from Korti since the 8th of January, over four weeks ago. Some time was spent calculating stores and making arrangements, the result being that 15,000 rations were left at the camp. There had been 60,000 rations at Gakdul, and quantities of ammunition, but of these only 30,000 rations and no ammunition were brought on to Abu Klea, and now 15,000 of these were to be left here; it certainly did not look like holding Gubat for any length of time, much more like a general retirement without even taking Metemmeh. The whole force moved off at two o'clock, and we halted at five on the edge of the scrub. There was to have been a rocket sent up from Gubat at eight o'clock, to show that all was still well; it never appeared, but as it was rather doubtful whether it could be seen at that distance, its non-appearance caused no anxiety. The only other excitement during the night was a wild Irishman of the 18th letting off his rifle at a bush, which he imagined to be the enemy; however, as the shot came from the direction of the 18th, we ascribed it rightly to heated Hibernian imagination, and did not put ourselves out about it.

We were off by 6.30 the next morning, and proceeded cautiously towards Gubat. On topping the low ridge that sloped down to the Nile, the column was halted to make a reconnaissance, but, nothing extraordinary being reported, it moved on again. A big flagstaff was the next object visible, that had not been erected before, and we were pleased also to see a vedette of the 19th at its base; so far so good, the garrison was evidently not in little pieces. Shortly afterwards, the low Guards' fort came into view, and close by it the remainder of the G.C.R., formed up for assistance in case we were attacked. In a few minutes we were there, and had been welcomed by the garrison, who were particularly glad to see the stores, as they had been on half rations the last five days. The only bit of news they had to tell us was the usual "shave" that the Mahdi was two days off with an army of 18,000 men. Whether that was so or not, I cannot say; but certainly at dinner that night was heard the noise of blank firing, big guns and rifles, in Metemmeh, which portended something agreeable to the enemy, probably reinforcements.

CHAPTER 20

The End of the Relief Expedition

There was a considerable squash in the fort that evening, but we all huddled up somehow, and got through the night in peace. Our only duty during the following day was making out camel-returns; and what with the deaths of so many, and many others having been lost or exchanged, and all being in an unfit state for work, it was some time before the camels could be apportioned to each company's satisfaction. Next came the orders for the whole of the wounded to be cleared out, and go to Gakdul before daybreak on the morrow; whether they could stand the journey or not was not the question. All were to go, the worst cases being carried on stretchers by a number of Egyptian soldiers, who had come with the last convoy.

As this looked still more like immediate evacuation, two or three of us went "down-town" to collect what we could in the shape of curios from the natives, and especially from Gordon's Soudanese, since we might not see them again. These latter inhabited an extraordinary little enclosure, called by courtesy a *zeriba*, about 200 yards off the river fort, and further upstream. They had been put there in order to prevent treachery or possible mutiny, and were thus well under the fire of both our forts. These precautions seemed unnecessary as far as the blacks were concerned, for they seemed thoroughly trustworthy, and anxious to stick to us, if only for the sake of plenty of fighting. Their officers, however, were a slippery lot, composed of Egyptians, Turks, Cypriots, Greeks, Bashi Bazouks, and the scum of all southern Europe. They were not to be depended on like the negroes, and a very small disaster would have turned their sympathies and services over to the enemy.

The interior of the *zeriba* was a wonderful sight. The whole place was filled with shanties made of poles and matting or ragged carpets, and inside these the blacks reposed, chattering, cleaning their arms, and swearing at their wives, who sat patiently outside cooking dinner. Every available space was occupied with arms, wooden bowls, grinding-stones, carcases of kids, cooking-pots, spears, corn, and ammunition-boxes. At the entrance a six-foot

INSIDE THE *ZERIBA*.

negro did sentry-go in a casual sort of way, whilst two piles of arms, with fixed bayonets, testified to the presence of a picquet somewhere; every ten minutes, too, a trumpeter blew calls of sorts on a huge key-bugle, but nobody seemed to pay any attention to them. Most of the blacks had arrayed themselves in blue jerseys and stocking-caps, whilst a good many wore regulation British trousers, with red or yellow stripes. On my asking where they got them from, they told me simply that they had walked about amongst the *Ingleez*, and taken whatever they could pick up. This propensity evidently accounted for many deficiencies in our weekly kit-inspections. They had not the smallest notions of *meum* and *tuum*; everything was public property, even amongst themselves. If you saw some quaint article lying about, and wished to possess it, the nearest person, whether he was the proprietor or not, would sell it to you and pocket the proceeds. They were very keen soldiers, and, if you made friends with them, nearly every one had a pet spearhead or sword, covered with dried blood and hair, which he produced out of some inner recess in his shanty, and showed with great pride. Although already armed with Remingtons, most of them had two or three spears or a sword to use at close quarters. Several of them were very keen to buy off me a particularly neat spear I had picked up. They balanced it, grinned, and showed a great liking for it, and even offered two spears in exchange. I don't know where the beauty of it lay; but, of course, seeing they appreciated it so highly, I declined to let it go. Eventually, after much haggling, we got several articles in exchange for some priceless cakes of tobacco, which the blacks valued far above money, and returned to our fort.

Before dawn next morning the wounded convoy paraded, but did not get off till daylight: they were escorted by some Heavies, Coldstream, Marines, and Mounted Infantry. The morning was occupied in getting our camels into decent order and feeding them as much as possible; for by this time it was no secret that we should evacuate the position and retire on Abu Klea as soon as all was ready. About noon a Hussar brought in word that the convoy was being attacked by the enemy, so we were for some time in momentary expectation of being ordered out to its assistance. Luckily, however, another messenger came in to say that the Light Camel Corps had come up in the nick of time from Abu Klea, and that the enemy had bolted. Thank God for that, as it might have gone hard with the wounded if they had had to wait till we could reach them on foot.

Parade had been ordered for inspection by the General at four o'clock, so we fell in completely equipped, in case we might have to start before nightfall. This was, however, not the case, and in the evening the whole force received orders to parade at five next morning to commence the retirement.

Now that our line of action had been definitely decided on,

the first thing to be done was to see that the column travelled as light as possible, for hardly any camels remained. Accordingly more than half the rations the last convoy had brought up were ruthlessly destroyed and thrown into the Nile. It was doubly irritating seeing these good things thrown away, since the garrison had been living on very short rations during the last ten days. 19,000 lb. of flour, 3,000 lb. of biscuit, 21,220 lb. of beef, 900 lb. of bacon, 1,100 lb. of tea, oatmeal, preserved vegetables, coffee, and all sorts of stores were pierced and thrown into the river. First of all, certainly, everyone was told to help himself to the good things, and was allowed to take as much in his private kit as he liked; but still it seemed a great pity that these rations, after having been brought at enormous trouble and expense from England, should, after all, only find a resting-place at the bottom of the Nile. There was no help for it, however; as it was, there were only just sufficient camels to carry three days rations to Abu Klea, besides one camel to every four men's kits. By seven o'clock that evening all the camels were watered and their loads ready for the start at daybreak; so we forgot our sorrows at mess in two bottles of fine old crusted (?) Tarragon port saved from the medical-comfort-boxes, and retired early to our last night's rest at Gubat.

Long before dawn the whole force was up, loading the camels and having their final meal. As bad luck would have it, the "casual" roster had just come round to my turn, and took me again for baggage guard, which included looking after the camels of the whole G.C.R. with their kits, since everyone was to foot it. One advantage I enjoyed, and that was the privilege of riding, for I could not possibly survey my forty-eight camels from on foot. By 6.30 the whole column was under way, and we moved out in broad column with our flanks well guarded in case of attack. This then was the end of the Gordon relief expedition! After all our fighting and losses we were to retire in this wise, having lost many valuable lives and much treasure, and gained absolutely nothing, thanks to the miserable vacillation and moral cowardice of Mr. Gladstone and the Radicals in not sending us out sooner.

CHAPTER 21

Retirement on Gakdul

It was a lovely morning when we left Gubat; rainless of course the weather always was, but this particular day strongly resembled early September in England, with white fleecy clouds floating about and a cool breeze from the north. It was first-rate weather for marching, and men and camels went strong and well till noon, when we halted for the rest of the day. Although the General had reason (and very good reason, as it afterwards turned out), to believe a strong force of the enemy was advancing from Khartoum, no Arabs were seen at all, and the afternoon was devoted to gentle slumber.

Nothing worthy of remark happened during the night, and by noon next day we had arrived at Abu Klea. There we found the Light Camel Regiment, and they gave us a more detailed account of the attack on the wounded convoy. It seems that the convoy was well inside the scrub when a large scattered force of the enemy was sighted through the long grass. Our force was then halted for defence, the Arabs closing in on all sides and doing considerable execution with their rifles. Owing to the broken nature of the ground hardly any enemy were visible to shoot at, and matters began to get serious. A Hussar was sent back at full speed to Gubat to acquaint Buller, and the fighting men were already formed into squares, flanking the mass of wounded, to await an attack, when suddenly a force of men on camels was seen in the distance, approaching from Abu Klea. Taking them for more of the enemy, the Mounted Infantry let fly a couple of long-range volleys at them—luckily without effect, for they turned out to be the Lights, arrived in the nick time. Seeing these reinforcements in their rear the Arabs all bolted, and the convoy was saved; so the whole pursued their way back to Abu Klea in peace. By the time we got there, the wounded convoy had already moved on towards Gakdul, together with most of the wounded left in camp.

General Duller had now arranged every detail of the retirement, and orders were issued for the Heavies, the 19th, ourselves, the Soudanese, and a convoy of stores, etc., to start next morning, all on camels, leaving the Lights, the remainder of the Mounted Infantry, and the 18th to keep the enemy in check till we could send back our camels to them from Gakdul. Owing to the want of reserve of camels at Korti, the rear-guard was thus stranded in the middle of the desert without means of transport or retirement in case of an attack by overwhelming numbers; if the enemy should attack, Duller was precluded from a fair fight on the open (again) by the want of transport for his wounded, so his only course was to "sit tight."

Most of the afternoon was spent in "taking over" camels for our start on the morrow; riding camels and baggagers had of course long ago got so mixed up that we took whatever came to hand. If possible, the poor brutes were in a worse state of decay than ever. I am afraid that by this time we looked on them as mere machines for carrying, and hardly thought of their sufferings from hunger and thirst as long as they could be whacked along. Eventually we were more or less suited with steeds, though certainly some looked as if they could not go another yard.

At six o'clock next morning our force started as ordered, and a curious sight it was. My post, in charge of that everlasting baggage, was just in rear of the Soudanese, and though the crowd of men and women were a great nuisance, getting in everybody's way and not keeping up, still one could not help laughing at the quaint sights. Here, a coal-black negress was perched on top of a camel (stolen of course), bestriding all her household goods and chattels in the shape of rags, bowls, carpets and pots, whilst her husband (or possibly owner) led the beast, or prodded it up with his spear from behind. There, an old man, who might have come from any nation under the sun, so nondescript was his colour and raiment, was trudging merrily along, his rifle slung over his shoulder and his spear-stick in his hand. Donkeys, too, were there in great numbers, each overburdened with his owner's goods. No sort of order was observed—negroes, Egyptians, women, camels, and donkeys all going their own pace, soldiers and slaves intermingled in wonderful confusion.

During that day we lost no less than ninety-two camels, which dropped from exhaustion and were left lying. If this sort of thing went on, we thought, there would be very few left to send back to Abu Klea, if any. Luckily, however, this excessive loss was not again equalled; it seems to have been rather the weeding out of the camels, for I do not remember more than thirty-five or forty giving up the ghost on any subsequent day. We halted that evening two miles south of Gebel es Sergain, and had a good night's rest till 5 a.m.

Getting off at 6.30, we had not gone far before Major M'Calmont passed, hurrying to Duller with despatches from Korti. He had several most interesting pieces of news to tell us, but could not wait to give us any details. Firstly we heard of the victory of the river column at Kirbekan on the 10th, and poor General Earle's death; secondly, what affected us even more, that Sir Herbert had succumbed to his wound and died the previous evening. It was a heavy blow to the whole force, for he was beloved and admired by every man in the column; we had hoped against hope, seeing him linger on week after week and finally start on his journey with the convoy. But it was not to be; the journey had dangerously increased his fever, and he had died just within sight of Gakdul. It was a personal loss to every one of us. It seemed only yesterday that he was riding about the column on his little bay horse, talking to everybody, with a cheery word or a bit of chaff for all, officer or man alike; his tall figure and yellow *puggaree* well known to every man in the force. Never a harsh word did he use; even on the trying morning before Abu Klea, as at all times, his orders were given (so to speak) good-naturedly, without fuss or hurry, and when he had made every arrangement necessary, he lit a cigarette and sat quietly down among us as if he was in his garden at home. Not to speak of his military talents and soldier-like qualities, he was *a real good sort*, and I don't know that higher praise could be given to anyone. The void it left in everyone's heart was very painful—a void nothing could fill; and for days afterwards I woke with a feeling of something *gone*. On hearing the sad news, the 19th Hussars, who had served under him in previous campaigns and were much attached to him, made a forced march in the hope of being in time for the funeral; but they arrived, unfortunately, just too late.

The third piece of news was that an expedition had been ordered to Suakin, to make a diversion on the enemy's flank, and, if possible, to reinforce us by means of a railway to Berber.

The latter part of this intelligence was received with open mouths and incredulous smiles. That a railway should be laid down across two hundred and forty miles of desert in time to transport troops to Berber to our assistance was rather too much to swallow. Even if there was an autumn campaign, the chances of which were just dawning on us, we very much doubted the possibility of making a railway across a rocky, un-surveyed desert, devoid of water and fuel, and crammed full of hostile Arabs, in time to be of any use; and as for making it in six weeks, why it was ridiculous! We also heard that this expedition was to consist of 10,000 men, including a brigade of Guards, another from India, and various regiments of the Line, besides the 5th Lancers and 20th Hussars. It was evidently going to be a big thing, and if successful in cooperating with us, meant that our campaign was only just beginning.

Later on in the day we met a water-convoy under Major Gould of the Lights, sent out from Gakdul to establish a water station near Gebel en Nus, to act as a reserve supply for Buller's force in case of emergency. The only contribution to us from Gould's convoy was our little friend Jacky, the spaniel (?), who was delighted to see us again, he having wisely retired from Gubat with the first convoy and taken up his quarters at Gakdul. On seeing his old friends he at once deserted and joined us, returning with us to Gakdul. The weather had been very cool all day, so much so, that on arriving at our halting-place I discovered I had worn my worsted sleeping-waistcoat during the march without noticing it. It was everything having such weather; the camels bore up better, and the men did not suffer in the least, although they had walked a long distance to ease their steeds. Our chief difficulty was our boots; both pairs had long since been worn out, and fabulous prices were offered for a new pair. During the ten days we had been quartered at Gakdul the rocks had cut them to ribbons, and now, more than six weeks after, there was hardly a respectable pair in the whole force. No shoemakers' tools or spare leather had been sent out, so the only way for us to repair them was to cut up old rifle-buckets, and tie the improvised soles on with string as best we could.

At noon on the 18th our force reached Gakdul; there we were to wait for the rest of Duller's column before retiring finally on Korti. By this time the wells were in a bad state; the two upper pools had been drunk down to the *animalculae*, and the camel pool was still worse. Several men had contracted typhoid, and altogether it was about time to quit the place.

On the evening of our arrival we got serious news: one of the correspondents came in and said that not twelve hours after we had left Abu Klea, a large force of the enemy appeared on the surrounding hills and began blazing away at the camp; he understood Buller to say that he wanted 300 troops back again, and his opinion was that we should all have to return the following morning. Luckily his opinion was not worth much, and, in the end, we got orders for only 100 men to hold themselves in readiness to escort a convoy back to Abu Klea on the following evening.

Next day, however, before they started, Major Wardrop rode into camp with consoling news: he and Tidswell of the M.I. and three mounted men had, by an exceedingly plucky and clever ruse,[1] succeeded in deluding the Arabs into a belief that a strong

---

1. He did not put it quite in this way!

force was taking them in flank; they had consequently bolted, and Buller was in safety. After all, only 100 men of the 50th were sent on with the empty camels, and the G.C.R. were informed that they would have to leave Gakdul next day for the wells at Abu Halfa, and encamp there pending Buller's arrival.

These wells were only some ten miles off, and from the description of them given in Fowler's map they sounded like Paradise—large open pools of water, plentiful vegetation, *dhoum* palms in hundreds, green grass growing all around, etc., etc. Although we had learnt that all beauties of nature in this part of the globe were to he taken *cum grano maxima salis*, still we felt that any variation from the eternal black rocks and yellow sand would be a relief, and looked forward to it accordingly.

CHAPTER 22

Robbers on the Road

As it happened, our journey was put off for another twenty-four hours, and we did not start till the morning of the 21st (February).

A short cut had been discovered over the hills towards Abu Halfa, and by taking this and making a bee-line towards a peculiarly-shaped hill on the horizon we soon arrived in the neighbourhood of the wells. The next thing to do was to discover the wells themselves, and this we did with the help of a very miserable, but polite, native we discovered in the grass, who, poor devil, would have done anything for a handful of *dhurra*. We looked in vain for the pools Mr. Fowler had promised, but did not see them; the only water being two or three little puddles about four feet square. One dilapidated palm was seen in the scrub close by, but that was all. Mimosa trees, however, flourished in abundance, and in a very short time the camp (such as it was) was pitched, and we prepared to make the most of our stay.

The first thing done, after posting sentries, was to build a *zeriba* of thorny bushes, enclosing the hospital tent, stores, and ammunition. This was to be used at night as a secure sleeping-place, while during the daytime we reposed under the mimosa trees close by. One of these was big enough to shelter the whole of the officers, and was accordingly used as the mess-tree; the rest of the men made themselves shelters with blankets, rifles, and bushes, and were very happy, having next to no work to do. As to the position itself, that was not quite as perfect as it might have been, owing to the formation of the ground. The water puddles were at the foot of the peculiar hill aforesaid, and within easy range of all the hills round, so we had to make the best of a bad job.

During the day pickets and sentries were posted on the hills, in such a position as to command the best view of the country, and to be able to give timely notice of the approach of an enemy from any direction. If we *were* attacked, the Arabs would most probably come from the north-east, for a track led that way through the hills in the direction of Berber, where we knew there was a strong force of the enemy. At night we had to be satisfied with a cordon of sentries all round the camp, sufficiently far out to give us time to form up if necessary. As another precaution, a heliograph was established on a hill two miles towards Gakdul, by means of which we could communicate with the force there under Sir Evelyn Wood; so, practically, we were as safe as was possible under the circumstances. The only unpleasant part would have been if the Arabs had lined the hills during the night, and potted us from there; happily they never did.

Once encamped, there was not much work to be done; the weather was already getting hotter, and there was very little to tempt us out of our comfortable quarters.

Our chief amusement lay in exploring the country after luncheon, for between nine and three any exertion in the sun was only productive of profuse perspiration. The day after we arrived several of us set out, per camel, to try and discover the wonderful paradise that Fowler had written about. As we got into the hills, a number of *wadies* and watercourses appeared on all sides, and it was difficult to decide which one to take. After following up several, which resulted in nothing (in the shape of water), we at length perceived a faint track here and there amongst the stones, and concluded to try that. Half a mile up this *wady*, Dr. Parke[1] (who had replaced Magill) and I came suddenly on a large pool of water hidden behind a steep rock, and the greener colour of the vegetation around pointed to more water underground. Another 600 yards over loose stones brought us to a similar pool;

---

1. Now out with Stanley's expedition (1888).

palms and green grass abounded close by, and the general effect was most refreshing. In the background the *wady* led into a sort of black gorge, bending round towards the south. This promised further interesting explorations, but we had had enough wandering about for that day; besides, if we explored everything at once, there would be no occupation for the rest of our stay. Accordingly we watered our beasts and ourselves, and returned to report. These two pools were each about twenty yards long by two or three yards broad sort of crescent-shaped and not more than three feet deep. Their value, however, consisted not so much in their size as in the fact that they proved the existence of water everywhere in the *wady*. Anywhere in the neighbourhood, if you scooped out a hole with your hands, it would rapidly fill with clear water, and go on doing so apparently *ad infinitum*. (If anybody wants to know why we did not remove the camp bodily to these pools, it was because by so doing we should have been more in a *cul-de-sac* than ever.)

The next few days were occupied in doing nothing particular, except building a small *zeriba* for some half-dozen bullocks and attenuated sheep we had been sent, as a great favour, by the Commissariat authorities. The cattle of the country seem to do without water nearly as well as the camels; they do not seem to mind going waterless for two or three days at a time, and keep up with a column on the march for 100 miles or more, subsisting on dry grass and one drink half-way. Naturally the beef suffers somewhat in quality and quantity; but though it may not always be equal to prime cuts from the sirloin, a fresh meat ration, such as it is, is very acceptable occasionally, as a variety from the eternal bully. Our beasts were no exception, and only had one failing, which I hope is not common to all Soudanese cattle: every night they used to butt away, or climb over, their thorny *zeriba*, and employ their keepers all day in looking for them.

Our other animals, the camels, were allowed to do pretty well what they liked, as a slight recompense for their previous sufferings. We had been allowed about eighty altogether (to some 220 men), and of these twenty at a time were kept tied up in case of emergency; the others roamed all over the country during the day, and were driven in at night. Even after three days there were visible signs of improvement; most of them began to fill out a bit, and got to look quite happy, but I grieve to say that Potiphar was an exception. He never seemed to stop eating, yet his ribs came as much through his skin after a gorging as they did before.

Near the camp we noticed tracks of various animals, chiefly gazelle and jackals, and used to wander out after them in the cool of the evening, though we rarely got anything. One thing struck me as rather peculiar, and that was the number of hoof marks all over the valley. We only had three ponies with us, belonging to three Hussars who were sent to help us, and we knew no Cavalry had passed that way, so I concluded they must be the tracks of Arab horsemen at some time or other. It was not long before we found out what they were.

One day, N—— and I started off on camels up the black gorge to explore, taking our rifles with us in case of game or niggers. It was very pretty when we got well inside. Patches of long green grass and rushes sprang up on either hand as we advanced, and the *dhoum* palms increased in greenness and size, showing up well against the precipitous dark rocks. Underfoot the sand showed signs of moisture, and every now and then a small pool glistened under some shelving rock there was water enough and to spare. Suddenly we caught sight of some forms moving about rapidly in the grassy tussocks ahead of us. "Gazelle!" whispered N——, and down we slipped, and tried to knee-lash our camels. Devil a bit; they wouldn't kneel on the nubbly stones, and stood there bellowing, enough to frighten any gazelle away for miles round. It was no good making more row than necessary, so I basely handed my camel to N—— to hold, and ran forward, keeping well under cover, to get a flying shot at the gazelle. They seemed very tame in fact extraordinarily so, for they were there still. I was just drawing a bead on the nearest beast through the grass, when suddenly he kicked up his heels, and bolted into the open, followed by the rest of the herd.

"Donkeys," I groaned, and returned to my camel, chastened in spirit. Alas! it was so; they were either wild asses, or else they had escaped from their native masters anyway, they wouldn't be caught, though we tried hard for more than half-an-hour. This evidently accounted for the hoof-marks.

Another ten minutes brought us to a large shallow pool, nearly covered with reeds and a sort of duckweed, where we found our three Hussars watering their horses; they had come round the other way on, for just here the gorge opened on to a clear space, which "gave" into the valley of Abu Halfa. Away to the north-east there was a cleft in the black hills, through which could be seen more *dhoum* palms, and lilac hills in the distance. It was very pretty. Close by was an extraordinary hill, shaped like a high pyramid, with a jagged natural breastwork on the top, and this did well as a landmark for the big pool. Round the pool were some shallow wells, with puddled troughs alongside in the sand; evidently the place was well-known to the natives round about, though we did not catch sight of any. As our further progress was barred by steep hills, we came straight back to camp, and told what we had seen.

Just about this time, reports came in of robbers on the road between Gakdul and Korti, who ill-used and robbed any single messengers who were being sent through. Worst of all, a wretched native, in charge of the homeward letters, was set upon one night in the dark, beaten, and robbed of his camel and mailbag. We were particularly annoyed; for, having nothing much to do, we had all written heaps of letters home. B—— had written nine and I five, and all the others several apiece; but there was no chance of any civilised person ever seeing them again. We soon got instructions, per heliograph, from General Wood at Gakdul, to send out camel-patrols by day and night, to search the road, and shoot or capture any outlying niggers we found. We caught none, for they kept well out of the way; but no more robberies were reported, for they had a wholesome fear of us.

Chapter 23

A Private Battle

Orders were daily expected from Gakdul for our return to Korti, and at length they came. Wood heliographed that we were to keep only forty camels in all to take us back, and that all the other camels were to be sent at once to Gakdul for transporting the sick and stores still there.

I happened to be next on the roster for "casual" duty, so accordingly started off in the evening with some forty loose camels, and ten men to escort and drive them. Luckily there was a moon about seven, and after various incidents, such as losing our way in the interval of darkness, and three camels departing this life, we got into the wells about eight o'clock. Just Before the turn in to Gakdul, I was riding in front, when I heard some extraordinary noises in the distance. At first I thought it was jackals, but soon the noises turned into a wild sort of moaning I could not understand. At length it dawned on me it was Arabs singing: if they happened to be the enemy, I thought, how on earth am I to keep forty straying camels out of sight of them in the moonlight? To my relief, they were only a party of friendly Kababish returning to Korti with a few Lights and stores, and they were as much surprised at coming across my party as I was at seeing them. Shortly afterwards we arrived at the Wells, and after a good feed with Nugent, we were all soon sound asleep.

Next morning I gave over my camels and started back, much reduced in numbers. The Wells had a very deserted look. Beyond the General, his staff, and some fifty men wounded or sick in hospital, there was hardly a soul there. The wells themselves were getting very unsweet, through the lowness of the water; the place bore every sign of a well-used camp, and it was high time to quit.

Halfway back, my advanced file reported Arabs ahead in the grass, and in truth, as I rode up, seven black forms armed with spears arose and scudded towards the hills. We pressed forward to cut them off, but our worn-out camels would not trot over the sharp stony ground, so there was nothing for it but to try to bag them somehow. I held up a white rag as a sign of peace; but they did not take to it kindly, for they halted a moment and then bolted again. This was evidently a sign of a bad conscience, so I dismounted four men, and gave them a couple of volleys at 900 yards. The range was capital, for I saw the spurt of the bullets close by them, and they ran—I never saw anybody get over the ground so fast—till they disappeared in the hills, and were seen no more. Shortly afterwards we met a small convoy going into Gakdul with empty camels, so I sent in a report of my battle to the General. All he said was, "It's a pity he didn't shoot them all."

On my return to camp, I found orders had been actually received (per heliograph), for us to start after Wood's column had passed the entrance to Abu Halfa Wells, three miles off. Wood was to start from Gakdul next evening (the 3rd of March) at five, so that meant we should pack up and go three or four hours after him.

Our camels were very limited in numbers and strength, one to every two officers, or every six men, and hardly any extra camels allowed for mess or otherwise. A supply of jams and pickles had at last arrived from Korti only two days before, and these we welcomed with rapacious joy; but if we weren't allowed any camels to carry these hardly-won condiments back, what was to become of them? Obviously only one thing—get through them as soon as possible, and bring back as much as we could carry privately. Accordingly, a quantity of these good things were distributed to the men, and after stowing away as

MY PRIVATE BATTLE.

much as we could in our kits, we stowed away the remainder in our stomachs. It was, in fact, a question of eating against time, hardly a useful preparation for a tramp of nearly a hundred miles. I heard some time afterwards that the Heavies had likewise been in much the same fix, having had several magnums of champagne sent them the very night after they left Gakdul for Korti. The friend in charge of the liquor, finding his camels requisitioned and the Heavies flown, thought it was a pity to waste good wine in the desert, so he packed what he could to take back on his own camel, and drank the remainder—two magnums—himself, at a sitting; good performance, I call it. The poor chap, Costello, of the 5th Lancers, died afterwards, though not from the champagne. A short time after the heliogram arrived, orders were issued, and the work of packing up our reduced kits and distributing the camels began. Everything had to be packed in the smallest space possible, and many were the growls at having to leave some treasured curio or trophy behind through scarcity of camels.

At last the welcome news came by flash, "Wood has just started." Thank goodness, we should get back to water and civilisation (more or less) in four or five days! As Wood's force would take at least four hours to get opposite Abu Halfa, and we wanted it to get well ahead before following, parade was not ordered till nearly daybreak.

There was a bit of a moon left still during the night, so we took advantage of it, and started about 3 a.m. What a falling-off was there! The last time we had passed along that track, it was in the full glory of a camel apiece, now there was barely one to every five men, and even these, poor brutes, were only kept on their legs by continual whacking.

The foot-gear of the G.C.R. was most extraordinary; the boots that had at length arrived from Korti, and which we had looked forward to as a real godsend, turned out to be of such small sizes that the men could hardly get their feet into them. They were as hard as bricks, there was no grease to soften them, and the only way of using them was to slit them open at the end, and shove your toes through. As for the officers, no two had the same foot-covering; field-boots, lawn-tennis shoes, gaiters, putties, and boots in all stages of decay and attempted repairs were worn. The men wore their black serge trousers, mostly tied under the knee like navvies', while several had lashed putties over them, and slit them at the thighs to allow of free ventilation. Others wore their old boots, with bits of leather tied on for soles. The *tout ensemble* was peculiar, though it might be workmanlike.

The first day's march was to be to Magaga Wells (at present occupied by the Heavies), distant some twenty miles off or more. Luckily, the sun was not very hot, and we plodded along cheerfully all day, stopping for a couple of hours at noon, to feed and rest. By five o'clock we had made Zobrick el Kelb, near which we were told the wells lay, and another fifteen minutes over piles of sharp stones brought us to the Heavies' camp. Here we were rejoiced by receiving a mail from Korti, and after a long drink and a good meal we were soon fast asleep.

Next morning we received orders to fill up water-tanks, to water the camels, and start that evening. I wanted to see what the wells were like, so, being off duty, I took a gentle stroll thither in the afternoon. It was an extraordinary sight. Following the stream of men and animals for half a mile, you came across a stony cleft in the hills which could hardly be dignified with the name of a ravine. It wound in and out between overhanging cliffs till suddenly you arrived at a large and dirty pool, where horses and camels were drinking. Above this again were crowds of men, buckets, pumps, and tanks, and at the far end of all these, in a dip overshadowed by perpendicular rocks 150 feet high, was a deep pool of water. These were the Magaga Wells, holding quite half the quantity of water as Gakdul; and why they had been only comparatively lately made use of, being so close to the track, I don't know.

That night, by eleven o'clock, before the moon was up, we had started on our way, and, with the exception of a rest of an hour for food during the small hours of the morning, walked all night till 7 a.m., when we arrived at the wells of El Howeiyat. Here there was a small detachment of Sussex to guard the wells and keep up the line of communication by signalling and otherwise. On the top of the hill above the wells was a heliograph, which could receive and flash messages all the way to Zobrick el Kelb on the one side, and Thirty-mile Hill on the other. Thus, by means of an instrument at Twelve-mile Hill and another at Abu Halfa, messages could be signalled straight from Korti to Gakdul in a very short time.

There we slept during the day, and moved off towards sundown, at 4 p.m. It was a curious foggy, murky evening; the setting sun beamed dimly through the clouds of dust, and we thought we were in for a regular *khamseen*. However, night went on, and the sky luckily cleared; we marched steadily ahead in the faint moonlight, and by the time the sun rose again, were within ten miles of Thirty-mile Hill, where there was a reservoir of water from Korti. Arrived at the camp, we got a good night's rest there; the following day we moved off in the early morning, and did about seventeen miles, bivouacking on the soft sand.

Next day, the 9th March, we passed Twelve-mile Hill early, and arrived within sight of the Nile and Korti about three o'clock. Not even Xenophon's Greeks could have been more delighted to see their sea than we to behold the prospect of unlimited drink, unlimited washing, civilisation, and tents. What a blessing it was getting to the Nile! Colonel Boscawen, L—— and D—— had arrived five days before, seedy, from Gakdul, and had got everything in order for our reception. After seeing to the men, N—— and I repaired to our mutual tent, and the joy of meeting one's spare baggage and a real bath was too great for words. Pyjamas, clean shirts, a new sponge (my old one was in rags), baccy, a complete change of attire, and a spare pair of boots it was delicious!

CHAPTER 24

Prospects of an Autumn Campaign

On arriving at the river, the first questions naturally asked were: "What is going to happen now? Are we really going to have an autumn campaign? Are we going to stick here all the summer, or are we going to quit at once?"

Nobody knew.

Wolseley was determined upon an autumn campaign, and getting to Khartoum, even though the main reason for the expedition was gone. The question was, "Would the country stand it?" We rather thought not; but still it was "on the cards," and meantime we amused ourselves by mild bets about whether we should be home for the Derby, for Lord's, for the 12th, or for next Christmas.

Two or three days followed of nothing in particular, except that we assisted the Heavies in finishing their champagne, which produced a curious effect in our unaccustomed heads. On the 10th, Lord Wolseley announced his intention of inspecting us, and did so, without many words, except that we were to stay up the Nile all the summer, and would probably advance again in the autumn.

The camp at Korti had assumed enormous dimensions during the ten weeks we had been away. What with the camps of the regiments who had arrived since the 30th December, and the quantities of stores that had been pouring in, it was hardly recognisable. We had left it a snug little place among palm trees, *dhurra* fields, and mimosa bushes; and now, behold, it was more like the Long Valley at Aldershot than a bit of the Nile. The camel lines were a mass of dust, the whole place was decidedly not as sweet as it was, and civilisation in the shape of a couple of Greek merchants had begun to intrude itself. It was time to move; the question was where to?

It was soon given out that directly the remainder of the desert force arrived (the river force having arrived on the 11th), the whole expedition would be distributed along the river for summer quarters. This looked like an autumn campaign with a vengeance; but still I for one did not believe that the British taxpayer in his cooler moments would sanction the cost of another expedition, and predicted we should be out of the country before June—which, as it happened, was not very far out.

Shortly after this announcement, orders were issued detailing the various quarters for the various regiments. Camps were to be formed at Merawi, Tani, Kurot, Dongola, and Hafir, and the big camp at Korti was to be entirely broken up, leaving only a small force of Soudanese blacks, these to be under the command of Commander J. Baker, R.N. We, the G.C.R., were destined for Dongola, there to remain till further orders. So far good. The Heavies were to make a camp forty miles north of that at Hafir, the 42nd Highlanders to form the advanced post at Merawi, the 18th (Royal Irish), the Mounted Infantry, and the 75th (Gordon Highlanders) to go to Kurot, the 50th (West Kent) and the 56th (Essex) to Tani, and the Lights to Shabadud; other arms, such as the 19th Hussars, Ordnance, Commissariat, and Medical Corps, Engineers, Artillery, and Egyptians, being divided up between these stations.

The hot weather being at hand, it was necessary to get to our respective stations and build camps there as soon as possible. Now that the river column had returned, we had all their boats to make use of in taking us down the river. Camels there were none left worth speaking of; the few that had dragged our kits back from Abu Halfa to Korti had been already sent back to help up the remainder of the desert force, and even they, poor brutes, were in such a condition of holes, maggots, and scragginess, that many of them never saw the river again. Alas, poor Potiphar! he must have been one of these, for, after bringing his share of kits to the Nile with us, he was sent back again, and though I made every inquiry afterwards about a big white camel, with a blue and white noseband, a vile temper, and a hole in his side big enough to put your helmet in, I never heard any more of him. Peace be to his bones!

The first to move were the Heavies, who, after having been in turn Cavalry, Infantry, and Mounted Infantry, now made their debut as boatmen. With about seventeen men and their kits to one boat, they paddled off on the afternoon of the 11th. Eight boats took the whole lot, a sadly reduced remnant of the magnificent corps which had started across the Bayuda. Out of 24 officers and 390 men, only 11 officers and 252 men were left, the remainder being killed, wounded, or sick.

We were under orders to start on the following day; without regret, therefore, we took over our thirteen boats, packed our kits and ourselves into them, and started in the afternoon with a gentle breeze from the north-east, which took us downstream at a good rate. Besides sixteen men and one officer, there were two Canadians to each boat, partly to teach us practical boating in the rapids, and partly to get them (the *voyageurs*) downstream as soon as possible, for their time of engagement was soon up. It was a beautiful feeling, sailing downstream in the cool of the evening like this, without a care, after our late toiling in the desert it was one of those things which ought to be felt to be appreciated.

At dusk we landed, not far from the future site of Tani Camp, and, running all the boats ashore, we bivouacked in great comfort on the sandy beach. Next day we were off by dawn, and, the northerly breeze still holding good, we made Debbeh by three o'clock. From here it was slower going, owing to the turn in the river, and the consequent unfavourable direction of the wind, so we had to get out our oars and pull. The men were in high spirits, and really enjoyed pulling; they looked upon it as a water-party, and several would not give up their oars when it came to their turn for being relieved, but insisted on pulling, for fun, they said.

The Canadians were stationed in the bows and stern, but

were not much use, as the river was simple steering and had few rapids just here. As a matter of fact, my boatmen spent most of their time asleep, with their legs hanging over the side. That night we spent at Kurot, here we found General Brackenbury and his staff superintending the laying out of the camp. The spot as close to Abu Gussi (the market town mentioned in a previous chapter), and was as desolate as any on the Nile. Its chief *raison d'etre* as a camping-ground lay in its sanitary claims, for it was an alluvial soil on a gravel bed whatever that may be. Be that as it may, I should not have been anxious to stop there a week, let alone three months.

Next morning we were off betimes, and, with a good breeze from the east, passed Shabadud and Handak about 10 a.m. The heat was already beginning to get unpleasant, and so were the flies at our midday meal. We did as much as we could that day, and encamped at a place about fourteen miles above Dongola.

That evening, as we lay comfortably in the sand after dinner, smoking our pipes before we turned in, two gigantic spiders made their appearance in our midst. Up we all jumped, over went lanterns and plates, and it was not till C—— had valiantly slain the beasts with a slipper that we ventured to return to our places. It's all very well to laugh and to treat spiders with contempt, but a bite from one of these brutes is no joke. Imagine a yellow brute with two pairs of beaks, a body rather longer than your thumb, and eight long red legs, covered with stiff and spiky red hairs, the whole beast barely to be contained in a soup-plate, and you have an idea of the apparitions which made for us that night. They devour little birds, their bite is by way of being poisonous, and they are horrible to look at. No wonder we bolted.

Insects of other sorts also began to multiply about this time. Every evening we liked to have a swim in the cool waters, but now it was fast becoming an impossibility. Millions upon millions of tiny sand-midges crowded the water's edge, especially in the neighbourhood of green stuff, and made bathing an infliction instead of a luxury. Luckily they disappeared with the sun, but ten minutes of their company every evening was enough to drive one wild with the tickling—they did not often bite.

Next morning we arrived in sight of Dongola—a good deal sooner than we expected—and disembarked at about ten o'clock. Our camp had been fixed for a spot over half a mile above the actual town, in a sort of enclosure formed by two *sakiyeh* troughs, running up from the river towards a collection of mud huts, some 200 yards back. In this space were already erected several large Indian tents, and the double bell tents we had brought with us from Korti were speedily put up for the men's shelter. As the daily-increasing heat would soon be too great for life in tents, the orders were that straw huts should be commenced at once, allowing twenty men to a hut.

Lord Wolseley was (supposed to be) going to make Dongola his headquarters, with General Duller as Chief of the Staff; but, besides his staff, part of the 19th Hussars, a detachment of the Sussex, and the Naval Brigade, there were going to be very few English troops there at all. In the place of troops was a huge Commissariat and Ordnance Store just above our camp; behind us, on the road leading to the town, was a portion of Egyptian artillery and cavalry, and scattered about near the stores were the tents of the C.T.C. and O.S.C.; subsequently came half a battery of R.A. and a half-company R.E. That was all.

For view from our camp we had a high bank of sand on the opposite shore, unrelieved by rocks or trees; the river itself was very low, and presented a very different appearance to what it did when we first came up. A broad sandy mud-bank reached nearly from shore to shore, leaving only a channel some fifty yards wide on each side of it. Just about here the river-bed was very wide, so that, the near channel being only half visible over the near bank, and the far one very nearly concealed behind the broad sand-bank in the middle, the Nile did not present that appearance of beauty which it should have. On our left were the hospital-tents, on the right some stray tents between us and the stores, and in our rear a few trees and mud-huts separated us from cultivated fields and the Dongola track: such were to be our quarters for an indefinite period.

CHAPTER 25

Life at Dongola

It would probably bore the reader even more intensely to read than it would myself to write what happened every day for the next three months, it was so very uninteresting. The fact was we simply vegetated, and with the exception of one or two little incidents that attracted our attention occasionally, nothing of any importance occurred till we went downstream for good and all.

As to work for the men, there was nothing to be done except building straw huts, and attending one parade a day. Since there was no material handy to make huts with, V—— D—— was told off, with a crew of eight men and the interpreter, to cruise about the river in a whaler, and buy poles and *dhurra* straw to make them with. The wily old Arab sheikhs had long ago made up their minds that the *Ingleezi* were sent by Allah solely for the benefit of their (the true believers') pockets, and accordingly charged outrageously throughout the country for the above-mentioned commodities, about two shillings per pole, and nine-pence per bundle of *dhurra*, being the prices demanded by the natives, and paid by the English authorities. Considering that each hut took about thirty-six poles and twenty bundles of straw to construct, the profit to the land in general must have been considerable.

For the benefit of future builders, I will endeavour to describe the huts, which were simplicity itself. A framework was made of poles about nine feet high, stuck into the ground so as to form a parallelogram thirty-two feet long by fourteen feet broad, and more poles were lashed across them at the top and half-way down. A puddled mud wall, eighteen inches high, was raised between the uprights, to keep the beasts and dust out, and the whole covered with straw matting. This last was made by a gang of natives out of the *dhurra* stalks we brought from the villages round.

Though it takes little time to describe them, it was more than four weeks before the men were under cover, and we (the officers) began building our own. Up to that time we were living in those capital little double Indian mountain tents, which let in plenty of air at night, and also plenty of sun in the daytime. Nothing but straw or mud kept that sun out it got stifling hot even in these tents, open at both ends, and right glad were we to get into our straw huts at last. We were not stinted in the way of room—only three officers to a hut, and with the interior divided by straw partitions every one had a cool room to himself.

Great was the ingenuity expended in architecting our huts, so as to get the maximum of shade and the minimum of heat. The chief drawback was that if you left any place open to the wind, which always blew (when it did blow) from the north or east, you were sure to be smothered in dust; if you didn't, you were stifled by the heat. Some of us rigged up doors of double matting; some put their doors on the wrong side. One started a three-foot mud wall to keep the dust out; somebody else made an extra door, and cross-barred it to keep the niggers (and himself) out, and let the air in, and I went the length of cutting a hole in my roof, and building a sort of lean-to over it; but the dust didn't seem to mind—it came in through the top as well as anywhere else, and so did the sun. We soon found it hopeless trying to keep an even temperature, so we made up our minds and perspired *ad lib*.

Our chief amusement during the cool of the day lay in exploring the town of Dongola, which, to tell the truth, had very little in it to repay our trouble. Imagine a plain town, about four miles round, and composed of one-storied mud-houses and narrow streets; round the outside, leaving a good space for cultivation between it and the town, a mud-parapet and ditch by way of fortification; one side of the town on the river, and on the land side a stretch of short green (?) turf dotted here and there with patches of cultivation, huts, and water-ditches; behind these again a desert of low, gray hills and nubbly stones, and you will have a good idea of our surroundings for three months. As for fine buildings and architectural beauties, there were none; a white plaster-faced barracks, a tumble-down old mud mosque, the palace of the Mudir (also made of mud), and a three-roomed white house belonging to an influential citizen and used as headquarters, were the only buildings that raised themselves above the level of the sea of mud huts of which the town was composed.

The main attraction was, of course, the bazaar, which was an unusually good one for the place. In it you could get every variety of fifth-rate French and Manchester cottons, cutlery, gimcrack stationery, and gaudy trash, but hardly any native work whatever. The chief things noticeable about the place were a very fine old fig-tree, and a greater tendency to lying and cheating among the merchants than anywhere else in Egypt, which is saying a good deal. There were two short covered places, and a small three-sided square giving on to a sort of Covent Garden market (I can't explain it any better), all full of shops *a la* Eastern, and a few stray ones besides, the whole thing covering about an acre. This description may seem rather wanting; but people who have seen it will, I have no doubt, recognise the place from it.

It was a sad disappointment not finding anything at all worth buying. Nearly everything came from Europe, the only native articles being those of consumption, and a few pieces of jewellery, generally rather ugly than otherwise. The silversmiths worked in a very primitive manner; in the first place, if you wanted them to make you something, say a bracelet, or a cigarette-case, you had to provide the metal to make it with, in the shape of *rials* or dollars. The operator threw the dollars into a crucible on a tiny fire, which a naked youth was pumping air into with a tiny pair of bellows, and that was all you could see that day. If you came back the following day, the chances were you would just miss the ten minutes the smith chose to work upon your article; it was no earthly use hurrying him he didn't understand it. If his ten minutes at it were over for the day, he would bring out the unfinished thing from his box and show it to you smiling; no threats or entreaties could make him go on with it till next day. He took at least a fortnight to do the smallest thing. When it was done, however, the result was often pretty; a quaint sort of filigree work was his forte, and how he managed to do it with his thick fingers and clumsy tools was always a mystery to me.

The prices were terribly high; at least they were to all the English. Acting on the old assumption that we were sent for their benefit, they charged us in dollars instead of shillings, and *piastres* instead of pence. If we would not give what they asked, somebody else would—it was all the same to them, and they made their profits accordingly. One particular scoundrel whom we patronised, by name Ali Shami, had a monopoly of fairly good European articles all the others were trash and bled us to such an extent that I expect by this time he takes his constitutionals in a carriage and pair of his own.

It was a quaint sight watching the natives in the bazaar. I used sometimes to spend the cool of an evening there, pretending to haggle with some blackguard for the price of one of his things, but in reality watching the people. I tried several times to sketch some peculiarities in costume or colour, but the attempt always came to grief. In the first place, an Arab's dignity is hurt if you stare at him; secondly, it is strictly contrary to his religion to have anything to do with pictures; thirdly, if you succeed in overcoming his scruples and getting him to sit to you, he is perpetually shifting his position or jumping up to have a look at the picture; and fourthly, a crowd of unsweet little boys, in every stage of undressedness, crowd round you and in front of you the whole time, entirely spoiling your temper and your picture. Having regard to these facts, I often wonder how it is that artists present you with a correct picture of an Eastern crowd or bazaar. I believe they do it from memory, helped by a vivid imagination. Do it on the spot you simply can't.

Every sort of nationality, colour, and tribe was united at Dongola. Greeks, Levantines, Cairenes, Portuguese, Abyssinians, Hindoos (in small quantities), Jews, Italians, and every variety of Arab, from the pale-faced Copt through the yellow mongrel and brown Bishari down to the Kordofani that you literally couldn't get any blacker if you were to polish him with a blacking-brush for a fortnight all—jostled each other in the bazaar. In the market outside sat crowds of women of all colours, each with several shallow round baskets of dates, vegetables, butter, or cheese in front of her—all talking at once. Especially was this the case on Thursday afternoons (their Saturday), when the noise really surpassed Whitechapel Road on Saturday evening.

Such was the place we visited every day during the first month of our stay.

CHAPTER 26

Dog-Hunting

As time went on, the bazaar began to grow rather insipid, and we cast about for other means of amusement. Bathing we had in plenty, for the 19th Hussars had erected a couple of header-planks opposite their camp, where the water was deepest, and hospitably told us to make use of them whenever we liked. The men, too, bathed every day, by order, just off our camp; but as the water never reached their shoulders there, those who could swim preferred enjoying a second dip in deeper waters.

Somewhat harder exercise, however, than promenading the bazaar was necessary to keep the men and ourselves from getting seedy; nothing damages you so much in a hot climate as having nothing to do, and plenty of time to do it in. Already several men were down with low fever of sorts, which developed itself into enteric in a few cases. We were getting flabby and slack with the heat.

The fact was we could not take violent exercise at any time of the day. The sun rose between five and six, and by seven o'clock it was too hot to attempt to go out without a helmet, or to exert oneself sufficiently to stir up the liver and get into decent condition. The only time for exercise was just before the sun went down till darkness came on, which it did much too quickly for our liking. Some of us used to go for long walks, some prowled about after birds and beasts, some tried fishing, but the amusement most patronised was riding.

By some means or other most of us had raised ponies; what with sales of effects of officers who had died or gone home, haggling with Arab horse-dealers, and requisitioning horses from the 19th Hussars on every available opportunity and for every conceivable purpose, the G.C.R. stud must have numbered twelve or thirteen animals, and, as may be well imagined, they were not allowed to run to flesh for want of exercise.

Dog-hunting was the best sport. Armed with long blunt sticks, the sportsmen in the whole camp assembled somewhere near the town, and proceeded to arouse some unfortunate slumbering pariah, and drive him towards the desert. Once his head was set desertwards, the whole field would *hurroosh* after him as fast as their crocks could carry them, and sometimes have capital sport. The idea was to charge him and knock him off his legs with your lance; but this did not always happen; to tell the truth, I don't remember ever seeing it done. The dog was generally too wily, and would dodge and bolt for the river or some friendly mud-hut, and there disappear. As he could turn much faster than any pony, he usually had six to four the best of it. No matter, there were plenty of dogs left; and after all, as long as you got a good gallop, what did it signify if you did lose half-a-dozen? I don't know why, but the bitches always gave us the best runs; when they once got their heads set for a point, they would go for it, and not condescend to twisting and turning: perhaps it was deficiency of brains, or want of presence of mind, or perhaps it was the desire to please common to the female sex; I don't know. They were real curs, most of them, and would yowl with fright if you raised a stick at them. One noble exception there was, who was run to a standstill miles out in the desert; he couldn't bolt any more, so he dashed at the legs of his solitary pursuer's pony. The sportsman hurled his stick at him and of course missed, so he generously turned his pony homewards and left the dog victorious, to get home that night if he could.

As regards shooting at Dongola, that was a delusion. Our most enthusiastic sportsman, D——, used to go out mysteriously at all hours of the day, and sometimes night, with a gun, his faithful servant behind him carrying his pea-rifle. He was generally late for dinner in consequence, and nine days out of ten his answer to our inquiries as to what he had shot was a cheerful "nothing." If he did bring anything back, it was usually only a few birds, such as red-breasted sparrows, green bee-eaters, and such like. These he skinned and kept. One day, however, he returned in great glee, dragging after him a big grey pelican he had shot with a rifle. The stench emanating from his hut for the next few days was something appalling. I assisted at the flaying thereof, and all went well till we got to operating on the head, and there we stuck; what was to happen to the great skin pouch under the beak? I forget how we squared it at last, but I know next day D—— called me into his charnel-house and pointed out in consternation that the pouch was turning dark red. By-and-by it got quite black, dried up, and finally began to split. I shall not easily forget D——'s anguish at this untoward occurrence; it seems he had destined the skin for the chief ornament of his paternal halls, and now his hopes were dashed.

The birds and beasts were not half so numerous or brilliant as we had expected to find. Beyond a very few gazelle, a few foxes, and plenty of lizards and chameleons, there were absolutely no four-footed animals; even crocodiles were at a premium, only one being bagged, by M——, during our stay. Some fifty miles down the river there were supposed to be four hippopotami, who had lived there for years; we organised an expedition for their slaughter, but, as it happened, it never came off. Birds were more numerous, but very sober in hue; besides the sparrows and bee-eaters above mentioned, I don't remember any brilliant-coloured ones. Hoopoes there were in plenty, and small wood-pigeons; but the other land-birds were as dingy as London sparrows and couldn't even sing. Among the water-birds, the razor-bill, a small black-and-white bird with a bill something like a toucan, was the most curious; and beside him there were a few pelicans, herons, paddy-birds wild geese and ducks, storks, and cranes, yet not in anything like the quantity we had been led to expect. Probably the advent of so many men and boats on the river drove the birds and beasts away, for further upstream, at Metemmeh, wild-fowl, black storks, adjutant-birds, and every sort of quaint water bird simply swarmed.

Fishing was a simple amusement—very—not requiring much skill on the part of the fisherman. When an Arab wants to catch a fish, he ties a strong hook on to a hank of cord, weights it with a stone and winds it onto a big reel with a big iron pin through the middle of it. He also provides himself with a little bell tied on to a thin stick. He then sticks the reel into the mud, and the bell-stick close alongside it, baits the hook with a lump of meat, takes a half-hitch round the bell-stick, throws the line into the river, and goes to sleep. If a fish gets hung on the hook, its struggles set the bell going: our friend wakes up, hauls in the fish, and repeats the process. The only difficulty about it is bringing the fish to land, and that is mainly a question of strength, for the Nile fish runs to an immense size. There seem to be only two varieties, one nastier than the other for eating purposes. The first rejoices in the Arabic name of *baggah* and looks like a big bream he is good as kedgeree, but not otherwise. The other one is a sort of *silurus*, thick-skinned, black and slimy, with a big flat mouth, and sort of antennae on his nose he is simply beastly to eat, specially at High Nile, when he tastes like solid mud.

We caught several of these brutes with night-lines, and would have caught some more, only our tackle always got stolen by some prowling nigger during the night. So we gave up that amusement in a very short time, and took to riding again.

CHAPTER 27

Conflagrations

Such was our everyday life in quarters, perspiring freely from seven to five, and then doing as much in the way of exercise as was possible till 7.30, when it got dark, and we had dinner. As regards our food, it was voted that three meals a day was too much for a hot climate, so they were reduced to two; breakfast at eleven, and dinner at 7.30. Soon, however, we began to discover an empty feeling in our interiors between sunrise and eleven, so we had a gentle *chota hazri* of tea and biscuits at 6.30 a.m., and, to fill up the gap between breakfast and dinner, another slight repast of the same about four; total, four meals instead of two.

The men had built us a capital straw mess-hut, and the greater part of the day we spent there, playing whist and piquet, and reading the papers, which were by way of coining once a week from England. As a matter of fact, the mails were often, I may say generally, two or three days late, owing to the dearth of camels and other means of transport. On one occasion the Mudir of Dongola, being sent downstream to Cairo, boned all the mail camels for his own private baggage and refused to give them up for some time. The river too was about as low as it could be, and the steam-launch that usually brought on the letters from Abu Fatmeh took to running aground on sandbanks, so the delivery was hardly as regular as it might have been.

Parcels came up occasionally, but they were even more erratic than the letters and newspapers, and many were the angry visits paid to the Dongolese Post Office. This was a dark, dirty room in the town, presided over by an impertinent little Italian, who kept the papers and parcels in such apparently hopeless confusion that it was wonderful how we got any letters at all. I remember getting very much annoyed with him one day, about some parcel I knew had arrived, and which he wouldn't produce, and I finished by threatening to report him to the Station Commandant. Imagine my indignation when next day I received a request from the Commandant to come and explain my conduct at the Post Office! The little brute had stolen a march on me, and reported *me* for using unparliamentary language!

Every day came in some new "shave," and the variety was nearly as great as it had been at Metemmeh. A telegram board had been put up in the middle of the camp, for official news and Reuter's telegrams, but it was much too scantily supplied for our wants. The main question, of course, was how long we were to stay up the river, and whether there would really be an autumn campaign. On this subject everyone had different views, and as everyone aired them as authentic on all occasions, the amount of rumours "on the best authority" multiplied exceedingly. Nothing was to be gleaned from the English papers. They had evidently forgotten all about us, and were crammed with nothing but leaders and articles on the new Franchise Bill, and such like matters of thrilling interest.

Reuter's correspondent was our best tipster, and he gave vent to some startling statements, mostly a little premature, which were believed as gospel. First, that the Cabinet had decided to evacuate the Soudan at once; then that it had cancelled its decision, and we were to go up to Khartoum, also at once; then that Wolseley had sent for exact states of the force, with a view to immediate action; then that we were to go downstream directly the Nile was high enough, and so on, *ad lib*. The chief outcome of these rumours was mild betting as to how long we should be in the country. I remember rashly laying three to one, which found ready takers, that we should still be at Dongola on the 1st of June; and a good bet it was. As it happened, we started downstream on the afternoon of that day, so I won my bets—but I am going ahead too fast.

One day (it was on the 7th of May) I was lying in rather a torpid state, as usual, in my hut, when I was aroused by a loud rushing and crackling sound just outside. I ran out, and beheld the windward hut of all a mass of flames. Not a second was lost; the whole camp was already turned out, and chains of buckets were rapidly organised to the river. But it was no use. Water had not the smallest effect on the flaming straw, and, one after another, six large huts were in a blaze. The whole thing did not take four minutes from the time the first hut caught till the last was a smoking heap, and next to nothing was saved. The Coldstream and Marines who were quartered in these huts escaped mostly in their shirt-sleeves; they had not time to get anything out, not even to put on their coats. As the bandoliers and pouches caught fire, *pop, pop* went all the cartridges, though happily no one was damaged by the bullets. By good luck, the sixth hut was divided from the rest by a big *sakiyeh*-trough on a high ridge of earth, so we were in hopes that the fire would not spread. Owing to the prompt arrival of the whole of the 19th Hussars with blankets not two minutes after the fire began, and the exertions of our own men, who covered the untouched huts with wet cloths and blankets, the fire was stayed. The only danger now to be feared was from the flying sparks, which were carried for many yards by the powerful wind, and, in one or two cases, alighted on other huts; but they were extinguished before they had time to do much harm, thanks to several sailors and others. Total damage: two companies of the G.C.R. left house-less and nearly clothesless. There was nothing to be done but to build the huts up again.

Chapter 28

Orders to Quit

Thus passed the time away, and very slow it seemed to us. There was great excitement about the Suakim campaign, and also about the Afghans and the Russians for a time, for we had it "on the highest authority" that war would be declared at once, and that we should proceed to the scene of action immediately. However, the feeling cooled down, as we realised there was not going to be war after all, and we cast about for new excitements.

Every Saturday, or thereabouts, the *Lotus*[1] used to pay us a visit from upstream, bringing down sick and taking back stores. She was a perfect boat for the river, and invaluable in the low state of the water, for even when fully loaded she only drew eighteen inches. Sometimes she brought a parson for Sunday services, though generally we did without one; and by her means we were kept *au fait* with what was going on upstream. Sometimes too, a few Mounted Infantry officers from Kurot, Lights from Shabadud, or Heavies from Hafir, would pay us a visit, and spend a day or two in the Dongola markets, buying provisions for their respective messes. Altogether, news circulated pretty freely along the river.

On one occasion we sent a picked crew of G.C.R. to try conclusions with the Heavies in whale-boat races. We were ignominiously defeated, but ascribed it to not knowing their course, and challenged them again. They came up to Dongola accordingly, and beat us again, by something like eight lengths. It

---

1. Stern-wheel Yarrow steamer.

is only fair, however,, to remark that our boat, the best we could get, was a square-sterned, broad-bottomed affair, which travelled woefully slowly, whilst they had the pick of the lot in the shape of something approaching a gig.

Not long after we had settled down at Dongola, an important addition arrived in the shape of Colonel Colborne, who had been acting as correspondent to the *Daily News* with the river column. He at once proceeded to make himself comfortable by hiring a house on the outskirts of the town close to the river, and mooring his private *dahabieh* alongside. Being of an antiquarian turn of mind, he somehow discovered that there were some remains of a temple four or five miles upstream, and resolved to dig it out. Accordingly, half-a-dozen of us accompanied him thither, on his *dahabieh* and in whalers, drank his brandies and sodas—such a luxury!—and pretended to be deeply interested in the proceedings.

To tell the truth, it was a curious place. The only outward signs of it at first were the broken tops of some stone pillars, all but buried in the sand. So we hired a lot of niggers, and set them to work with shovels. Very soon the pillars began to grow, and the niggers found themselves on the roof of a tiny temple. Digging away all round this disclosed some interesting hiero-glyphics on the walls, and seven or eight feet down we came on some large figures in relief of gods and goddesses, together with the top of the entrance into the holy place. As enough had been done for one day, we returned home, intending to come another time. It so happened that a strong wind blew for the next three days, and when we returned to the place nothing was visible but the broken pillar tops as before—all our labour was buried in the sand-drift! As we had no guarantee that the wind wouldn't do it again, we didn't try again, and left the sands their secret. The only other things near the place were dozens of little green copper gods and goddesses strewn about; it must have been a god-foundry in its day, for in some places there were hundreds of broken crucibles and pieces of pottery, and bronze rings, and things green with age. I also picked up a transparent lizard with big eyes (alive), and what rather astonished me was that he fell off his tail, leaving it curling and wriggling in my hand. I tried to join him and his tail again, but some sand had got in between and it wouldn't stick, so I left him looking forlornly at it.

The 19th Hussars used to have every week a Friday afternoon "at home," where all sorts of sports were indulged in. Tent-pegging, melon-cutting, bare-backed races, musical rides (without the music), hurdle races, flat-races, camel-races, all had their day. Some of the sporting Arabs used to enter their horses in the flat-races, the *Vakeel* (head man of the town now that the Mudir was gone) especially being a great owner, and also jockey. One particular race was a great favourite; it was riding bare-backed a short distance round a post, coming back to the starting-post, dismounting, sitting on a chair, drinking a bottle of ginger-beer, and then the course again. Another one was tandem-racing, riding one pony and driving another. All this took place on "Newmarket Heath" at the back of the town, a magnificent stretch of ground, called by courtesy turf. Though perhaps not so green as it might have been, it made a first-rate racecourse, and many were the Friday afternoons we attended this Gymkhana meeting.

To chronicle all the interesting events that occurred along the river, race-meetings, concerts, and general news, I——, the enterprising adjutant of the G.C.R., started a newspaper. It contained a vast amount of interesting information, scientific, sporting, social, and otherwise, and was printed by the Engineers, who had brought up a printing-press amongst other useful things. It was called the *Dongola News*, appeared every Saturday, and did a wonderful trade. The pity was it didn't begin its career soon enough, for it only reached its fourth number.

May was drawing to a close, and, though we did not know it, the day was approaching for going downstream and leaving the charms of Dongola for ever. The news had got abroad amongst the natives that the English were going to quit, and great was the confusion that ensued. Facilities were offered to the inhabitants in case they wished to go downstream too, and everyone took advantage of the offer. Proclamations were issued that the English Government had decided not to hold Dongola longer than was absolutely necessary, and that in fact all British troops would be withdrawn as far as Wady Halfa or thereabouts. The immediate result of this was that a general exodus of the natives began. Everyone bolted as if the Mahdi were at his heels. Streams of niggers and Arabs, men, women, and children of all shades gathered together their goods and chattels and flocked out of the town. The only check put on their flight was that they should keep to the west side of the river, and not interfere with the retirement of our troops. At first it was laughable to see these poor panic-stricken people making their way downstream, they were in such a hurry to get away; but very soon it became rather a nuisance than otherwise. The town and villages near became entirely deserted, and the bazaar from having been a lively scene of crowding natives and colours got to look simply wretched. Day by day the stalls emptied, and at last not a soul was left in it. Nothing but old wrappers and dirty pieces of paper littered the ground, and, bar the regulation curs prowling around, not a living soul was to be seen—it was quite depressing. There was not the smallest need for such haste, for the 42nd had not yet left Merawi, and even if the whole of the English had been already withdrawn below Debbeh, there was no enemy to speak of this side of Berber; however, the niggers seemed to think so, and went accordingly. Where these poor people all went to, I don't know. The richer ones and merchants I suppose went into Lower Egypt with their ill-gotten gains, and either pursued their callings there, or retired to live in ease forever after; but the poorer ones, the peasantry, must have had a hard time of it, as I know the natural river-bank inhabitants do not take kindly to newcomers.

By the time all the inhabitants had left the district, news came that the 42nd had actually left Merawi (the most advanced post of all), and were on their way downstream in whalers. The next to move were the Soudanese at Korti, then the camps at Tani,

Kurot and Shabadud in succession, and eventually we were to break up and go, leaving the 50th West Kent (from Tani) in our places as rear-guard.

On the 30th May the 42nd passed Dongola, aided by a strong south-easterly wind, which came in very much *a propos* (and as a matter of fact precipitated General Buller's arrangements rather too much for his liking.) *At last* we got our orders to start in the 50th's whalers directly they arrived: with this wind it would probably be in two days. A great relief it was knowing this for certain, or at all events knowing that we should be out of this part of the country before many more weeks were over. There were not many preparations to be made. Furniture, mess-huts, beds and benches we left for the 19th or 50th, and of luggage we had not very much. There was no one left to say goodbye to, and all we had to do was to sit and wait for the 50th. The last evening

I spent on Colonel C——'s hospitable *dahabieh*, but beyond falling into the Nile on the way back to camp I do not remember much about it.

Chapter 29

Wady Halfa

The 1st of June dawned (and I had won my bets). It was an awful day, worse than any we had yet had. The wind blew hard from the south-east, and with it clouds of black dust which made us long for the appearance of the West Kent. By telegram we heard that they and the South Stafford had left Shabadud on the previous day, so they ought not to have arrived before evening. However, the wind blew them downstream a grand pace, and they appeared about two o'clock.

It did not take long for them to get themselves and baggage out, or for us to take their places. Before the sun was down we were well beyond Dongola, skimming along at a rate that would take us about three times as fast as the authorities had intended. As we sailed along, straggly caravans of unfortunate natives and their goods were seen making their way down country on the left bank. The villages along the river had a painfully deserted look, and it was sad to watch the "families-removing" process going on from them.

That night we encamped on the bank, and slept in the soft sand. Our marching was to begin next day at Abu Fatmeh. The days of camels were over, alas! and nothing remained but to get ourselves home by ordinary civilised means as quickly as possible. The G.C.R. had long ceased to be a Camel Regiment, and we were once more to be real genuine Infantry.

It was very sad to compare our present state with what we were seven months before, going up country. *Then* each man had a camel of his own, real breeches and putties, and a respectable grey tunic; now every man was reduced to his own legs as transport, khaki trousers much too short for him, and a badly-fitting khaki tunic. *Then* the G.C.R. was over 400 strong, with every hope for the future; now the object for which we came was gone, and there were 90 of us gone also. The Heavies had, however, suffered far worse. Out of the 24 officers and 430 men who had come up, only 8 officers and 210 men were returning. Burnaby, Gough, Atherton, Law, Darley, Carmichael, and Wolfe had been killed; St. Vincent had died of his wounds, Browne and Costello from enteric fever, and Somerset, Beach, Binning, Gore, and Murdoch had been sent home wounded or invalided. Of ourselves, thank goodness, no one had died; Crutchley, Poe, and Magill had been sent home wounded, and Townshend, Drummond, and Baden Powell invalided but that was all. Dongola was to be abandoned, and all our troops withdrawn below Wady Halfa no chance of an autumn campaign. It was very hard lines to leave the country thus in the hands of the Mahdi and his followers, and we felt that the native confidence in England was rudely shaken. However, if the British tax-payer wouldn't stand another expedition, he wouldn't, and there was an end of it.

The morning after leaving Dongola the boats flew down the river before the wind, and we must have done the distance to Abu Fatmeh in record time. It was rather ticklish work steering through the miniature rapids which appeared now and then. Especially irritating was it, on taking a shot at one of two channels, to find your whaler grounding on the sand and rocks in the wrong one. With wind and current dead against you it required a good deal of hard pulling to get back and turn into the right one. The Nile was very low, and with sandbanks and islands appearing in mid-stream, it was a toss-up as to which channel between them was shallow and which deep. Luckily no serious mishaps occurred, and our fleet arrived at Abu Fatmeh Camp about midday.

Somehow the wind did not seem to act on shore, for it was frightfully hot directly we landed. We were stowed away in straw rest-huts till the evening, when we were to begin our march, and the temperature was like a furnace. It was higher than we had ever had before 122 degrees in the shade. Glaring hot rocks and no trees to speak of were the *spécialtiés* of the place, and we thanked our stars we were to be off the same day.

Just below Abu Fatmeh was the cataract of Kaibar, and here the river took a long detour. The orders were therefore to send our baggage round through the rapids in boats, and take a short cut across country to the Kaibar Camp.

A detachment of Kroomen had been sent up from the Mediterranean squadron to do the piloting of the cataract, and extraordinary people they were. Their dress was supposed to be that of an English blue-jacket, but the varieties of clothing were endless, from a loin-rag upwards. Coming from the West Coast of Africa, they were a different type of negro altogether from the Soudanese, and had a break-jaw lingo of their own that nobody could understand. This latter difficulty, however, made little difference to them, for they jabbered broken English (very broken it was, too) with the greatest pleasure. Each Krooboy was borne on his ship's books under an English Christian and surname, such as Tom Teapot, Uncle Fat, Salt Pork—anything that was in his sponsor's mind at the time of christening. They were very cheery fellows, and certainly wonderful at getting a boat through an impossible place.

To these men we confided our baggage, M—— and P—— being sent with them to superintend, and started on our walk as the sun was setting. Every one of us was in shocking bad condition for a tramp after our long stay at Dongola doing nothing, and before we got to Kaibar next morning the want of training began to tell. The distance was by way of being seventeen miles, but I made it twenty-three, if not more. However, a beautiful wash and drink in the river put us right in no time, and, after resting in the camp during the day, we started again in the evening.

During the next week the programme of getting downstream was the same. Rest-camps had been organised all down the river, wherein we were to stay during the heat of the day; the marching always took place at night. Starting about 6 p.m., we marched for three or four hours and then bivouacked in any handy place, slept till 2 or 3 a.m., and then off again, arriving at the rest-camp just when it was getting hot. The pleasantest part of the day's work was arriving in the morning hot and tired and plunging straight into the Nile it was beautiful. In the more unfrequented parts there were a good many water-birds, and many was the stalk I had after them, always without result. It was very pleasant wading after storks and cranes, up to one's neck in water and with nothing on but a helmet and an eye-glass, but somehow the birds were shy. They always chose the moment to flap away just when the water was so deep that you couldn't use your rifle, and though they settled again a hundred yards further on, I, for one, never succeeded in getting a comfortable shot. D—— was so keen to get another big bird, as a *pendant* to his pelican, that he'd wander after birds in a hopeless sort of way for hours. Once a flock of cranes led him out of sight altogether, and he missed the turning into the rest-camp and wandered on twelve miles or so to the next; but never a feather did he get.

AFTER WATER-BIRDS.

Crocodiles there were also; occasionally one of them would be aroused by our splashing and slide out into deeper water, but nobody ever got a shot at one.

The rest-camps we passed the daytime in were composed of half-a-dozen large straw huts for us, and a couple of tents for the officer in charge of the station. They were all very much alike, and with no particular features to remember them by, except that at Koyek, where I remember there was a comfortable mud-house and a big mud-mosque, with Grenfell of the 10th Hussars in command. The names of the camps from Dongola down to Wady Halfa were as follows: Abu Fatmeh, Kaibar, Dulgo, Absarat, Saad Effendi, Koyematto, Ushematto (somebody shot a sand-grouse here with a rifle—browned a covey sitting), Koyek, Abri, Sarkamatto, Dal, Akasheh, Tanjour Road, Ambigol Wells, Rail-head, and Wady Halfa, but I have no distinct recollection as to what the first seven or eight of these were like; suffice it to say they were all in palm-groves on the bank of the river.

Whilst we walked thus, our baggage went by boat, and some-times caught us up at the halting places; generally it didn't. Any-way, it didn't matter, as cooking-pots and blankets came along with us on a camel or two, and the baggage was sure to turn up somehow. Some donkeys and a couple of ponies came too, be-sides a *cacolet*-camel for anybody who fell sick, so that the small column was well provided with transport.

From Abri to Akasheh we went by boat, each in charge of a pair of Krooboys. It made my hair curl passing some of the rap-ids, but only two of our boats got stove in a little after all. The Dal cataract between these places had too little water for boats to pass, so we went round it on foot.

At Akasheh we left the river, not to see it again till Wady Hal-fa. Tanjour Road lay eleven miles on in the desert, and here we found Surtees of the Coldstream (and at that time of the Egyp-tian army) with a rest-camp, and a few Egyptian soldiers and camels to supply it with water from the river four miles off.

In the evening the Egyptians held some athletic sports for our benefit. The great feature of the sports was boxing-matches *a la* Egyptian. This meant you might hit your adversary anywhere you could, and if you took his wind so much the better it was easier to knock him down so. There was not very much science about it, but the "Gippos" seemed to enjoy the fun immensely, and came up smiling time after time. Leap-frog was another item on the card, and the Egyptians ran about like a lot of boys just let out of school—I had no idea there was so much fun in them.

BOXING *A LA* EGYPTIAN.

At last we turned into the hammocks provided for us, and slept in the blissful consciousness of approaching comforts. The half-battalion of Coldstream and Marines had been sent off in the afternoon to Ambigol Wells and Railhead, twelve miles ahead, so as to get into the train first thing in the morning, and we were to follow them at about twelve hours interval.

Accordingly next morning at 4 a.m. we started, and, arriving at Railhead about ten, we welcomed the sight of a real train with effusive joy. Gangs of Indian coolies were laying the track, and we thought ourselves back in the heart of civilisation. We were to go by train to Wady Halfa, some fifty miles on, and there we ought to have arrived about 6 p.m. or so. However, a "scratch" railway in the middle of the desert is not quite the same as an English one, and at six we found ourselves not halfway, at Ambigol Road. Here we met a lot of hospitable Transport and other officers, nearly all of whom we knew. During an excellent tea of cake and drinks we exchanged ideas, but there was not much of importance going on, except the sending of troops down the river "hard all." Amongst other items of news we were told that Townshend of the Marines, who had been sent down from Dongola with enteric fever, had become much worse at Wady Halfa, and was dead. The sad news gave us all a tremendous shock. He was going on favourably when we had heard of him last, and we proceeded to feel dismal about it. Luckily the report turned out to be unfounded, but this we did not hear till we got to Wady Halfa.

It was far into the night when we arrived, and most of us were pretty cramped by that time—eight of us in a tiny guard's van for seven hours was rather a tight fit, especially as there were no seats; but that was quite a detail. Our attention had been taken off the squash by the heavenly feeling of being in a real live train again! It was a distinctly bumpy train, both in its mode of progress and the number of knots in the floor; but it was lovely all the same. The feeling of skimming along over stony tracks it had taken hours, even days, to plod over on camelback, really brought home to us the blessings of civilisation in a solid form.

Chapter 30

Alexandria and Home

On arriving at Wady Halfa we found a couple of *dahabiehs* awaiting us, and orders to start next morning; so we got out of the train and went on board for the night. On the following day we got parcels upon parcels of clothes, tinned meats, games, and every sort of thing that had been sent out to us and stuck on the way. Upstream these articles would have been most useful; as it was, they only added to our baggage. H—— and I wandered about on shore, and we had breakfast at a restaurant. Fried potatoes! white table-cloth! china cups and saucers! it almost took away our breath—the magnificence of the surroundings. I then went to see poor Townshend in hospital, and after some time was admitted. I never saw such a change. Although he was certainly not looking fit on leaving Dongola, I had no idea he would be so altered—so weak he couldn't sit up, so thin you could almost see through him, and his complexion a ghastly dark blue. His grave had already been dug for him; but he happened to hear of this interesting fact and vowed he wouldn't fill it, and he didn't. He gradually mended, and is at this moment in one of the crack native Indian Cavalry Regiments.

Eventually we got off in our *dahabiehs*, being tugged downstream by a steamer; but we didn't get far. Two hours after starting the big *dahabieh* stuck on a sand-bar, and no efforts on our part could get her off again. So there we lay all night, and next morning sent our steamer back for a *dahabieh* which would draw less water. As our boat drew seven feet, and most of the sandbanks were only four feet below water, it is not surprising that we stuck. It was tiresome being stopped like this, for the 75th Gordon Highlanders were close behind, and, as there were very few steamers to take all the troops down, it was a case of first come first served.

For the next fortnight we bumped downstream, often aground and hardly ever two nights running on the same boat. Sometimes they shifted us on to steamers, at other times we were jammed up in small *dahabiehs*, but the method of proceeding was pleasant and not fatiguing. For want of something better to do we took to shaving off our beards, and one after another apparent stranger came up from below minus the chin-covering that had graced (?) his face for the last nine months. It is extraordinary how a beard alters the whole face. Parke, our doctor who replaced Magill, we had never seen clean-shaved, and when I had helped him to carve the hair off, I literally had to introduce him to the others. They thought he was an intruder of some sort.

Occasionally, in fact very often, one of the boats stuck, and then everybody, stripped to his helmet, waded out and hauled away till something happened, either the rope broke or the boat moved. The pilots seemed to be trying how many sandbanks they could run us onto in a given time; hardly a day passed without our striking on something.

Towards sunset every evening the *dahabiehs* or steamers anchored, as it was impossible to pilot in the dark, and then was the time for a beautiful swim. The Arab sailors used to climb on to the paddle-box with their patches of carpet, turn their faces to the East and say their prayers, and it gave me extreme pleasure to take a header off the paddle-box just in front of them. They got awfully annoyed at a dog of a Christian getting between them and Mecca, as they had to begin their prayers all over again, and at last they took to cursing me in the most approved style; but it apparently had no effect.

The first important place we touched at was Korosko, where the 79th (Cameronian) Highlanders. were quartered. It seemed a regular suntrap to live in. High rocks on all sides and hardly a scrap of vegetation anywhere. The desert road (225 miles) to Abu Hamed starts from this point, and that was I suppose the reason for having a regiment there. There was not the slightest chance of being attacked that way; but still important information came sometimes across that fearful desert, one of the worst in the Soudan; so it was necessary to intercept it.

Assouan was reached on the 19th June; but, although we stayed there a couple of days, there was nothing worthy of note. Four days more brought us to Edfou, a lovely temple with vast stones for a roof—don't know how the Ancient Egyptians got them there—saw it by moonlight and two days more to Luxor. Here we stopped for a day, and went to see all the ruins; these I won't try to describe, as "Murray" knows a good deal more about them than I do.

At last, on the 29th, we got to Assiut, the head of the railway from Cairo, and on the following afternoon were entrained for Alexandria. We were not to halt at Cairo for long, but only to stay for breakfast, and then push on as fast as possible for Alexandria.

The train reached the Boulak Dacrour station [Cairo) at about nine, and there we found a sumptuous breakfast prepared for us. Every sort of good thing was provided, down to real ice for everybody. This 1ast was a great luxury, for we had naturally seen lone since the previous October. I believe, as a matter of fact, one block of ice used to be sent up weekly to Dongola from Alexandria, for the use of the patients in hospital; but, as may be imagined, it was rarely bigger than a walnut when it arrived; generally there was only past evidence of it in the shape of damp sawdust.

It is curious how you can do without the everyday luxuries of a hot climate when you haven't got them. We used to swallow all our liquids lukewarm up the Nile and never thought of cooling them. Tepid water, very slightly cooled in *chatties*, was the order of the day, and nobody dreamt of grumbling about it. Once, at Dongola, we got hold of some champagne, so, to keep up the civilised custom of drinking it cold, we hung it in the sun in a wet sock all day, and really the coldness of it gave me quite a shock I'd got so used to tepid drinks. I verily believe a lot of the sickness at Suakim was owing to the ease with which you could procure ice there at all times of the day. However, to return.

On the platform was the whole Headquarter Staff, including Lord Wolseley and General Stephenson, and one or two real English ladies, and delighted we were to see them all. One great disappointment we suffered here, and that was to hear that there was to be no separate medal for the Nile expedition—nothing beyond the old blue and white Egyptian thing with one clasp for the whole expedition, another for the desert column, and another for the river column, so those who had already the medal were to have only two clasps for the whole thing! We had had faint hopes that they might possibly give us a star (like that given to the troops in the Kandahar march) for the desert fighting, but were not prepared for the crushing news that we were not even to have a distinct decoration of any sort. It seemed rather curious to wear the old medal with the sphinx and "Egypt" on it for work not done within hundreds of miles of Egypt, for Egypt stops at Wady Halfa! However, there was no help for it. I heard more than one man say when he heard the news, "Blow me then if I ever volunteer again for this sort of business," and several re-echoed his opinions. This is a sore subject, so I'll drop it.

The entertainment at Boulak Dacrour did not last long, and within the hour we were steaming away for Alexandria. Luckily the railway arrangements were in a fitter state than when we were on the way up country, and we arrived within sight of the deep blue sea by four o'clock. The orders were to go on board the *Australia* (P. & O.) at once; but we were not to start for England for another three or four days, as various arrangements were pending.

The first thing we found on the quay was the brigade of Guards that had just come from Suakim, and had put in to Alexandria on the way to Cyprus, and very glad we were to see them all again, though some were utterly unrecognisable at first in beards. They were all in a disgusted state, first at being sent to Cyprus for an unlimited time, and secondly at being sent to dawdle at Alexandria on the way; however, we cheered them up, and for the next five days had a very pleasant time of it in the town. At last came definite orders to start, and on the 4th July we left Alexandria and the shores of Egypt for good.

Appendices

APPENDIX I.

COMPOSITION OF THE CAMEL CORPS.*

I. HEAVY CAMEL REGIMENT.

Staff.

Lieut.-Col. Hon. R. Talbot, 1st Life Guards, in command.
Captain Lord St. Vincent (K), 16th Lancers, Adjutant.
Surgeon J. J. Falvey, A.M.D., Surgeon.
Lieut. G. Leigh, 1st Life Guards, Acting Quartermaster.

DRAWN FROM	OFFICERS COMMANDING DETACHMENTS.	SUBALTERNS.	N.C.OS.†	MEN.
1st Life Guards	Major Hon. C. Byng	Lieut. Lord Rodney	5	38
2nd ,, ,,	Captain Lord Cochrane	,, R. J. Beech (w)	5	38
Royal Horse Guards (Blues)	Major Lord A. Somerset (w)	,, Lord Binning	5	38
2nd Dragoon Guards (Bays)	Captain A. L. Gould	,, R. F. Hibbert	5	38
4th ,, ,,	Captain J. W. Darley (K)	,, C. W. Law (K)	5	38
5th ,, ,,	Major W. H. Atherton (K)	,, [St. J. Gore]	5	38
1st Dragoons (Royals)	Major W. Gough (K)	,, J. F. Burn-Murdoch	5	38
2nd ,, (Scots Greys)	Captain W. H. Hippisley	,, R. Wolfe (K)	5	38
5th Lancers	Major L. Carmichael (K)	,, H. Costello (w.D)	5	38
16th ,,	Major T. Davison	,, W. B. Browne (D)	5	38

† Including 1 Trumpeter per detachment.

* Those officers whose names are in brackets were unfortunately prevented by sickness from crossing the desert. (K) after a name = killed, (w) = wounded, (D) = died of disease.

189

2. LIGHT CAMEL REGIMENT.

Staff.

Colonel Stanley Clarke, h.p., in command.

Captain H. Paget (w), 7th Hussars, Adjutant and Quartermaster.

Surgeon P. B. Connolly, A.M.D., Surgeon.

DRAWN FROM	OFFICERS COMMANDING DETACHMENTS.	SUBALTERNS.	N.C.OS. †	MEN.
3rd Hussars	Major C. E. Beckett .	Lieut. J. S. Scott .	5	38
4th ,,	Captain C. W. Peters	,, R. Kincaid-Smith	5	38
7th ,,	Lieut.-Col. H. McCalmont	,, Hon. R. Lawley	5	38
10th ,,	Lieut.-Col. J. P. Brabazon	,, Hon. G. Bryan .	5	38
11th ,,	Major C. E. Swaine .	,, W. Harrison	5	38
15th ,,	Captain A. G. Holland	,, P. K. Coke .	5	38
18th ,,	Major C. O. Gould (D)	,, E. G. Knox .	5	38
20th ,,	Captain E. R. Courtenay .	,, R. M. Richardson	5	38
21st ,,	Major W. G. C. Wyndham	,, J. Fowle .	5	38

† Including 1 Trumpeter per detachment.

3. GUARDS' CAMEL REGIMENT.

Staff.

Lieut.-Col. Hon. E. E. Boscawen, Coldstream Guards, in command.

Lieut. C. Crutchley (w), Scots Guards, Adjutant.

Captain E. M. Crabbe, Grenadier Guards, Acting Quartermaster.

Surgeon J. Magill (w), Coldstream Guards, Surgeon.

Lieut.-Col. H. Bonham, Grenadier Guards, Chief Signalling Officer.

DRAWN FROM	OFFICERS COMMANDING DETACHMENTS.	SUBALTERNS.	N.C. OS.†	MEN.
1st Bat. Grenadier Guards	Lieut.-Col. C. R. Rowley	Lieut. Count A. E. Gleichen.	5	38
2nd ,, ,, ,,	Lieut.-Col. I. C. Herbert	,, L. D'Aguilar	5	38
3rd ,, ,, ,,	Captain E. M. Crabbe	,, R. Wolrige-Gordon	5	38
1st ,, Coldstream ,,	Lieut. V. J. Dawson	,, Hon. H. Amherst	5	38
2nd ,, ,, ,,	Lieut.-Col. F. Graves Sawle	,, D. Dawson	5	38
1st ,, Scots ,,	Lt.-Col. Sir W. Gordon-Cumming	,, [B. Baden-Powell]*	5	38
2nd ,, ,, ,,	Lieut.-Col. M. Willson	,, [A. Drummond]*	5	38
Royal Marines ,,	{ Major W. H. Poë (w) Captain A. C. Pearson	,, C. V. Townshend ,, H. N. White	9	93

* Replaced at Gakdul 13th January, 1885, by Lieut. F. Romilly, Scots Guards.   † Including 1 Bugler per detachment.

4. Mounted Infantry Camel Regiment.

Staff.

Major Hon. G. H. Gough (w), 14th Hussars, in command.

Captain J. H. Sewell, Norfolk Regiment (9th), Adjutant.

Lieut. R. A. Grant, Gordon Highlanders, Acting Quartermaster.

Majors { Major C. T. Barrow, Scottish Rifles (26th & 90th).
Captain T. H. Phipps (D), 7th Hussars.

A Company.

Captain C. H. Payne, Gordon Highlanders, commanding.

		N.C.O.	PTES.	FORMERLY
South Stafford-shire Regt. }	Lieut. C. O. Hore	... 5	...25	...38th & 80th.
Black Watch ...	„ C. P. Livingstone (w)	5 ...25	...42nd „ 73rd.
Gordon High-landers ... }	„ H. K. Stewart	... 5 ..25	...75th „ 92nd.
King's Royal Rifle Corps }	„ P. S. Marling, V.C. } „ R. L. Bower }	5...25...	60th.

B Company.

Captain H. A. Walsh, Somerset Light Infantry, commanding.

		N.C.O.	PTES.	FORMERLY
West Kent Rgt...	Captain A. T. Morse	... 5	..25	...50th & 97th.
Sussex Regt. ...	Lieut. F. G. Todd Thornton	5...25	...35th „ 107th.
Essex „ ...	„ R. J. Tudway	... 5	...25	...44th „ 56th.
Duke of Cornwall's Light Infantry }	„ C. G. Martyr	... 5	...25	...32nd „ 46th.

C Company (Rifle Company).

Captain R. S. Fetherstonhaugh, K.R.R. Corps, commanding.

			N.C.O.	PRIVATES.	FORMERLY
K.R.R. Corps.	Lieut.	A. E. Miles (w) ...	5	... 25	60th.
K.R.R. Corps.	„	W. P. Campbell ...	5	... 25	60th.
Rifle Brigade	„	Hon. H. C. Hardinge	5	... 25	Rifle Brigade.
Rifle Brigade	„	W. M. Sherston ...	5	... 25	Rifle Brigade.

D Company.

Captain C. B. Pigott, 21st Hussars, commanding.

			N.C.O.	PTES.	FORMERLY
Somerset Light Infantry.	Lieut.	T. Snow (w)	5	...25	13th.
West Kent Regiment ...	„	E. A. Alderson	5	...25	50th & 97th.
Connaught Rangers ...	„	C. J. Carden	5	...25	88th & 94th.
Royal Scots Fusiliers ...	„	H. S. Stanuell	5	...25	21st.

A proportion of buglers is included in the above details.

TOTAL.

	OFFS.	N.C.O. & MEN.
Heavy Camel Regiment	24	... 430
Light „ „	21	... 387
Guards „ „	23	... 403
Mounted Infantry Camel Regiment... ...	26	... 480
Grand Total ...	94	... 1700

APPENDIX II.

CAMEL EQUIPMENT.

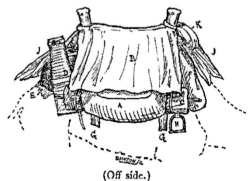

(Off side.)

A.   Zuleetahs (red leather and white canvas).

B.   Saddle-cover (red leather).

C.   Rolled blankets and tente d'abri.

D.   Namaqua rifle-bucket (brown leather), with strap to fasten on the near side.

E.   Water-skin (dark brown), resting on a yellow leather flap.

F.   15 lb. bag of corn.

GG. Girths.

H.   Stirrup.

JJ. Protecting flaps of red leather.

K.   Small red cushion—use doubtful.

The near side is very similar, the roll corresponding to C consisting of the great-coat and waterproof sheet, whilst the mussek (long Egyptian water-bottle) hangs in the place corresponding to that occupied by the rifle-bucket.

The girths are separate from the saddle, and pass over the framework. At one end of the girth is an iron ring, at the other a strip of leather. Each is simply fastened by knotting the strip of leather on to the iron ring on one side of the camel.

The stirrup-leather is either nailed on or hung round one of the bars of the framework.

APPENDIX III.

CAMEL DRILL.

Regiments will form up mounted one camel's length from front to rear rank. Men fall in with advanced arms. Companies told off as follows:

Number —, left of right half company.

Numbers —, —, —, —, left of sections.

Right half company, trail arms; left half company, trail arms.

Outer sections, advance arms; inner sections, advance arms.

(Sections right wheel, if further proving is necessary.)

The movements executed by Infantry by fours will be done by sections. When movements are not feasible by sections they will be done by files (front and rear rank men abreast) or by single file.

As a rule, when mounted, march in half-distance column; when about to dismount, if in column, the word "close order" will be given; close on the leading company as close as possible.

POSITIONS FOR DEFENCE.

On the word "dismount" the column will dismount, and, leaving the camels double knee-lashed, will form up in half-column* in the following positions, according to the word of command. Flanking squares can thus be formed:

Position 1. Half-column to right front.
,, 2. ,, ,, left ,,
,, 3. ,, ,, right rear.
,, 4. ,, ,, left ,,
,, 5. ,, ,, right front and left rear.
,, 6. ,, ,, left ,, and right ,,
,, 7. Square round camels.

* "Half-column" means column of companies at half-company distance, and *not* half a column.

195

Positions 1, 2, 3, 4, will be taken up as follows :—

Half-column formed on the right flank will be in column by the left.

     ,,   ,,   ,,   left   ,,   ,,   ,,   right.

Half-column to the right or left front will be formed on the markers of the rear company.

Half-column to the right or left rear will be formed on the markers of the front company.

The officer who places the marker upon whom the other markers cover, will take care that the half-column is as near as possible to the camels, the faces of the square (when formed) in every case being at the same time clear of the camels.

Positions 5 and 6 :—

Half-column at opposite angles will be similarly formed, and if the battalion consists of eight companies the leading half-battalion will form the front square, and the rear half-battalion the rear square.

In positions 5 and 6, when the battalion is composed of four companies, column of half-companies should be formed at either point, and not half-column of companies.

In all cases when the regiment is dismounted, a certain number of men will be left among the camels.

(*a*). When it is *not* intended that the half-column shall move from the camels two men will suffice as guard.

(*b*). When it *is* intended that they move from the camels, and if there is a co-operating body affording protection to the camels, two men per company will be left, but in this case the guard will have an officer.

(*c*). When the column is to move away, and there is no co-operating body of troops, an officer's guard of a quarter the force will remain ; its first duty will be to see that the camels are well secured.

Position 7. Square round the camels.

The leading company forms up in front of the centre of its camels, and the rear company in rear of the centre of its camels.

The odd companies (3, 5, and 7), will form up on the right flank of the camels.

The even companies (2, 4, and 6), on the left flank.

The companies on the right and left flanks will regard themselves as shifting bodies, intended, in addition to protecting the flanks, to join the companies on the front and rear faces.

[Thus, suppose the commanding officer to give the word, "Half-column on the left front," when the battalion of four companies is moving (on camel-back) in column of companies. The command immediately follows, "Close order." The leading company halts at once, the rear rank jams up close, and all the other companies trot up "hard all." When well jammed up against the company in front of them, the men dismount amidst a diabolical bellowing and grunting from their steeds, and double-knee-lash them with the head-rope. You then have all the camels in a square mass, unable to get up or move about. The right markers of companies having handed over their camels to be lashed by one of the two men ordered to remain with the beasts of each company, dash out, and are covered at half-company distance from the rear, the men running out and forming up on them at once ; they are then ready for forming square or other manœuvre. The same holds good for the other three corners, the directing flank always being nearest the camels. If the word is given, "Square on left front," the men run out to their places in square at once. For squares at opposite corners, four half-companies run to each place mentioned. When the battalion is required to manœuvre away from the camels, one company or less is left to defend them. In the case of two or more battalions the masses are formed in the same way in *échelon*, so as to cover each other.]

APPENDIX V.

LOSSES OF THREE CAMEL REGIMENTS IN THE CAMPAIGN.

1. HEAVY CAMEL REGIMENT :—

	OFFICERS.				MEN.			TOTAL LOSS	
	KD.	WD.	DIED.	KD.	WD.	DIED.		OFFS.	MEN.
1st Life Guards ...	0	0	0	... 2	0	2	...	0	4
2nd „ „ ...	0	1	0	... 2	0	3	...	0	5
Blues	0	1	0	... 1	4	4	...	0	5
2nd Dragoon Guards	0	0	0	... 5	1	2	...	0	7
4th „ „	2	0	0	... 7	5	1	...	2	8
5th „ „	1	0	0	... 10	7	1	...	1	11
1st Dragoons ...	1	0	0	... 12	4	3	...	1	15
2nd „ ...	1	0	0	... 11	5	4	...	1	15
5th Lancers... ...	1	1	1	... 5	4	5	...	2	10
16th „ ...	1	0	1	... 4	1	3	...	2	7
Total	7	3	2	... 59	31	28	...	9	87

2. Guards' Camel Regiment:—

| | | OFFICERS. | | | | MEN. | | | TOTAL LOSS. | |
		KD.	WD.	DIED.		KD.	WD.	DIED.	OFFS.	MEN.
1st Grenadiers	...	0	0	0	...	2	5	1	... 0	3
2nd ,,	...	0	0	0	...	1	1	3	... 0	4
3rd ,,	...	0	0	0	...	1	4	2	... 0	3
1st Coldstream	...	0	0	0	..	3	2	5	... 0	8
2nd ,,	...	0	1	0	...	4	7	1	... 0	5
1st Scots ...	...	0	1	0	...	3	2	2	... 0	5
2nd ,, ...	...	0	0	0	...	3	5	2	... 0	5
Marines ...	...	0	1	0	...	9	12	7	... 0	16
Total ...	...	0	3	0	...	26	38	23	... 0	49

| | | OFFICERS. | | | | MEN. | | | TOTAL LOSS. | |
		KD.	WD.	DIED.		KD.	WD.	DIED.	OFFS.	MEN.
3. Mounted Infantry Camel Regiment }		0	5	1	...	11	67	(?)	... 1	(?)

ALSO FROM LEONAUR
AVAILABLE IN SOFTCOVER OR HARDCOVER WITH DUST JACKET

DOING OUR 'BIT' *by Ian Hay*—Two Classic Accounts of the Men of Kitchener's 'New Army' During the Great War including *The First 100,000 & All In It.*

AN EYE IN THE STORM by *Arthur Ruhl*—An American War Correspondent's Experiences of the First World War from the Western Front to Gallipoli and Beyond.

STAND & FALL by *Joe Cassells*—A Soldier's Recollections of the 'Contemptible Little Army' and the Retreat from Mons to the Marne, 1914.

RIFLEMAN MACGILL'S WAR by *Patrick MacGill*—A Soldier of the London Irish During the Great War in Europe including *The Amateur Army, The Red Horizon & The Great Push.*

WITH THE GUNS *by C. A. Rose & Hugh Dalton*—Two First Hand Accounts of British Gunners at War in Europe During World War 1- Three Years in France with the Guns and With the British Guns in Italy.

EAGLES OVER THE TRENCHES *by James R. McConnell & William B. Perry*—Two First Hand Accounts of the American Escadrille at War in the Air During World War 1-Flying For France: With the American Escadrille at Verdun and Our Pilots in the Air.

THE BUSH WAR DOCTOR by *Robert V. Dolbey*—The Experiences of a British Army Doctor During the East African Campaign of the First World War.

THE 9TH—THE KING'S (LIVERPOOL REGIMENT) IN THE GREAT WAR 1914 - 1918 by *Enos H. G. Roberts*—Like many large cities, Liverpool raised a number of battalions in the Great War. Notable among them were the Pals, the Liverpool Irish and Scottish, but this book concerns the wartime history of the 9th Battalion – The Kings.

THE GAMBARDIER by *Mark Severn*—The experiences of a battery of Heavy artillery on the Western Front during the First World War.

FROM MESSINES TO THIRD YPRES by *Thomas Floyd*—A personal account of the First World War on the Western front by a 2/5th Lancashire Fusilier.

THE IRISH GUARDS IN THE GREAT WAR - VOLUME 1 by *Rudyard Kipling*—Edited and Compiled from Their Diaries and Papers Volume 1 The First Battalion.

THE IRISH GUARDS IN THE GREAT WAR - VOLUME 2 by *Rudyard Kipling*—Edited and Compiled from Their Diaries and Papers Volume 2 The Second Battalion.

LEONAUR

ALSO FROM LEONAUR
AVAILABLE IN SOFTCOVER OR HARDCOVER WITH DUST JACKET

WAR BEYOND THE DRAGON PAGODA by *J. J. Snodgrass*—A Personal Narrative of the First Anglo-Burmese War 1824 - 1826.

ALL FOR A SHILLING A DAY by *Donald F. Featherstone*—The story of H.M. 16th, the Queen's Lancers During the first Sikh War 1845-1846.

AT THEM WITH THE BAYONET by *Donald F. Featherstone*—The first Anglo-Sikh War 1845-1846.

A LEONAUR ORIGINAL

THE HERO OF ALIWAL by *James Humphries*—The days when young Harry Smith wore the green jacket of the 95th-Wellington's famous riflemen-campaigning in Spain against Napoleon's French with his beautiful young bride Juana have long gone. Now, Sir Harry Smith is in his fifties approaching the end of a long career. His position in the Cape colony ends with an appointment as Deputy Adjutant-General to the army in India. There he joins the staff of Sir Hugh Gough to experience an Indian battlefield in the Gwalior War of 1843 as the power of the Marathas is finally crushed. Smith has little time for his superior's 'bull at a gate' style of battlefield tactics, but independent command is denied him. Little does he realise that the greatest opportunity of his military life is close at hand.

THE GURKHA WAR by *H. T. Prinsep*—The Anglo-Nepalese Conflict in North East India 1814-1816.

SOUND ADVANCE! by *Joseph Anderson*—Experiences of an officer of HM 50th regiment in Australia, Burma & the Gwalior war.

THE CAMPAIGN OF THE INDUS by *Thomas Holdsworth*—Experiences of a British Officer of the 2nd (Queen's Royal) Regiment in the Campaign to Place Shah Shuja on the Throne of Afghanistan 1838 - 1840.

WITH THE MADRAS EUROPEAN REGIMENT IN BURMA by *John Butler*—The Experiences of an Officer of the Honourable East India Company's Army During the First Anglo-Burmese War 1824 - 1826.

BESIEGED IN LUCKNOW by *Martin Richard Gubbins*—The Experiences of the Defender of 'Gubbins Post' before & during the sige of the residency at Lucknow, Indian Mutiny, 1857.

THE STORY OF THE GUIDES by *G.J. Younghusband*—The Exploits of the famous Indian Army Regiment from the northwest frontier 1847 - 1900.

LEONAUR

ALSO FROM LEONAUR
AVAILABLE IN SOFTCOVER OR HARDCOVER WITH DUST JACKET

WELLINGTON AND THE PYRENEES CAMPAIGN VOLUME I: FROM VITORIA TO THE BIDASSOA *by F. C. Beatson*—The final phase of the campaign in the Iberian Peninsula.

WELLINGTON AND THE INVASION OF FRANCE VOLUME II: THE BIDASSOA TO THE BATTLE OF THE NIVELLE *by F. C. Beatson*—The second of Beatson's series on the fall of Revolutionary France published by Leonaur, the reader is once again taken into the centre of Wellington's strategic and tactical genius.

WELLINGTON AND THE FALL OF FRANCE VOLUME III: THE GAVES AND THE BATTLE OF ORTHEZ *by F. C. Beatson*—This final chapter of F. C. Beatson's brilliant trilogy shows the 'captain of the age' at his most inspired and makes all three books essential additions to any Peninsular War library.

NAVAL BATTLES OF THE NAPOLEONIC WARS *by W. H. Fitchett*—Cape St. Vincent, the Nile, Cadiz, Copenhagen, Trafalgar & Others

SERGEANT GUILLEMARD: THE MAN WHO SHOT NELSON? *by Robert Guillemard*—A Soldier of the Infantry of the French Army of Napoleon on Campaign Throughout Europe

WITH THE GUARDS ACROSS THE PYRENEES by *Robert Batty*—The Experiences of a British Officer of Wellington's Army During the Battles for the Fall of Napoleonic France, 1813.

A STAFF OFFICER IN THE PENINSULA *by E. W. Buckham*—An Officer of the British Staff Corps Cavalry During the Peninsula Campaign of the Napoleonic Wars

THE LEIPZIG CAMPAIGN: 1813—NAPOLEON AND THE "BATTLE OF THE NATIONS" *by F. N. Maude*—Colonel Maude's analysis of Napoleon's campaign of 1813.

BUGEAUD: A PACK WITH A BATON by *Thomas Robert Bugeaud*—The Early Campaigns of a Soldier of Napoleon's Army Who Would Become a Marshal of France.

TWO LEONAUR ORIGINALS

SERGEANT NICOL by *Daniel Nicol*—The Experiences of a Gordon Highlander During the Napoleonic Wars in Egypt, the Peninsula and France.

WATERLOO RECOLLECTIONS by *Frederick Llewellyn*—Rare First Hand Accounts, Letters, Reports and Retellings from the Campaign of 1815.

Lightning Source UK Ltd.
Milton Keynes UK
UKOW03f2303070414

229570UK00001B/169/P